"This book has the rare
substance, and practical
read for mothers of you

—Susan Alexander Yates, author,
And Then I Had Kids and *Then I Had Teenagers*

Do you feel like you are carrying the *mother* Over-*load?* Then take a break and refresh yourself with the book you are holding in your hands. Mary's suggestions for meeting your needs will be like a drink of cool water—a blessing to both you and your family!

—Kendra Smiley, conference speaker and author,
Aaron's Way: The Journey of a Strong-Willed Child

I've always wished I had a smart, kind mom living next door who could give me advice, reassure me that I'm not crazy, and help me to handle the mother load. This book is the next best thing to that mom next door. Mary Byers offers friendly, practical advice on caring for yourself while caring for others. She reassures us moms that it is not just okay to take care of yourself, it's essential, and she offers wise and very practical counsel on just how to do so.

—Keri Wyatt Kent, author,
God's Whisper in a Mother's Chaos and
The Garden of the Soul

Want to be a more balanced, joyful, playful and sane family manager? Join Mary Byers—a real mom like you and me—on an enjoyable journey of unloading the heavy stuff and replacing it with all that's good and rewarding and fun about motherhood.

—Lorilee Craker, author,
*We Should Do this More Often: A Parent's Guide to Romance,
Passion, and Other Pre-Kid Activities You Vaguely Recall*

Who better to encourage moms toward personal growth, while commiserating about the lack of available time, than a mom in the trenches? Mary Byers speaks to our heartfelt needs with humor and understanding born of experience. Moms seeking practical ways to balance their responsibilities should put down their mother loads and pick up this book!

—Cynthia Sumner, author,
Mommy's Trapped in the Bathroom

Mary Byers makes us feel valuable and understood through her compassion, humor, and willingness to share her own joys and frustrations of motherhood. Reading *The Mother Load* is like sitting across the table from Mary, drinking a cup of coffee or having milk and cookies. She is friend, cheerleader, and mother extraordinaire.

—Leslie Levine, author,
Wish It, Dream It, Do It

Moms will be encouraged, refreshed, and find their "mother load" and hearts lightened by Mary Byers' new book *The Mother Load*. With both inspiration and practical ideas, I highly recommend it to moms of all ages!

—Cheri Fuller, speaker and author,
The Mom You're Meant to Be

The Mother LOAD

Mary Byers

HARVEST HOUSE PUBLISHERS

EUGENE, OREGON

Published in association with the literary agency of Alive Communications, Inc., 7680 Goddard Street, Ste #200, Colorado Springs, CO 80920.

Cover by Terry Dugan Design, Minneapolis, Minnesota

Cover photo © Regine Mahaux/The Image Bank/Getty Images

THE MOTHER LOAD
Copyright © 2005 by Mary M. Byers
Published by Harvest House Publishers
Eugene, Oregon 97402
www.harvesthousepublishers.com

Library of Congress Cataloging-in-Publication Data
Byers, Mary M., 1962–
    The mother load / Mary M. Byers.
        p. cm.
    Includes bibliographical references.
    ISBN 0-7369-1502-8
    1. Mothers—Religious life.   2. Motherhood—Religious aspects—Christianity. I. Title.
    BV4529.18.B94 2005
    248.8'431—dc22   2004017414

Printed in the United States of America

    06 07 08 09 10 11 12 13 / VP-KB / 10 9 8 7 6 5 4 3 2

In loving memory of my niece,
Skyler Nicole Carlson,
October 5, 1999–August 28, 2002

Dedicated to my grandmother,
Mary Marguerite Kierspe,
who encouraged my love of books;
and my mother,
Nancy Kierspe Carlson,
who gave me a love for words.
From them I'm also learning the gentle art
of handling the mother load.

Acknowledgements

I've been blessed with wonderful family, friends, and great influences in my life, many of whom have encouraged me and prayed for me as I wrote this book. If you're one of them, thank you.

I especially want to thank Nancy Carlson for being an excellent mother and encourager. I inherited any ability I have with words from her, and I appreciate her understanding of, and enthusiasm for, this project.

My mother-in-law, Phyllis Byers, taught me early on that family comes first. I've absorbed the lesson. Thanks for welcoming me into *your* family.

My stepmother, Cari Carlson, accepted the Herculean task of parenting another person's children, and she did so creatively and patiently. My brothers and I benefited. Thank you Cari, for all that's gone before and all that is yet to be. In addition to caring for us, I really appreciate how well you take care of Dad, too!

I wouldn't have had the chance to write this book if it weren't for the Hearts at Home Publications Team, led by Mary Steinke and comprising Tonya Irvin, Megan Kaeb, Jill Savage, Holly Schurter, and Becky Wiese. Though I haven't met all of you personally, I'm indebted to you for seeing something in the kernel of the idea I first presented to you. My literary agent (I love writing that!), Chip MacGregor, was next in the line of encouragers. I look forward to many years of working with him and enjoying his sense of humor.

Special thanks to the two small groups I've been privileged to be a part of at my church. One has been meeting for over a decade, and one I've just been a part of for a short time. We've seen each other through some serious times, and I'm so grateful to have fellow believers to walk life's path with. Bless you.

My friends, whether mentioned by name in this book or not, have blessed my life immensely. Thank you.

Tara McAndrew and Julie Kaiser, my writing buddies, kept me going even in the midst of uncertainty. And I appreciated the trips we made to Incredibly Delicious to enhance our creativity. Leslie Levine, author and muse, shared her experience with me openly and freely. Everyone needs a mentor like her! Marie Prys served as a sounding board, second set of eyes, and encourager. Thanks for your willingness to work with me. To Barb Eimer: Thanks for being my friend for all these years. Keep writing!

The Harvest House staff has exceeded my expectations. Thanks to LaRae Weikert for seeing something in this manuscript; to Betty Fletcher for shepherding it through the production process; and to Barb Gordon for the love and attention she gave this project. A special thanks to the Harvest House staff who have supported me, but who I have not yet met at the time of this writing. I'm so thrilled to be working with you!

As you'll see at the end of each chapter, dozens of women took the time to respond to a survey about "the mother load" and have let me include their thoughts, ideas, and observations in this book. I gained valuable insights while reading these comments, all of which were sincere and heartfelt. I was reminded how difficult life can be, but heartened by the energy and enthusiasm with which we women approach the challenges that come our way. If you were one of the many women who shared your heart with me, I'm grateful to you.

Perhaps the biggest thanks of all goes to my husband, Stuart, for allowing me the freedom to write this book and making motherhood possible for me, and to my children, Stuart Jr., Marissa, and Mason. Without you, there would be no *Mother Load*, and there would definitely be less joy in my life.

Contents

Meeting Your Need for...

1

Meeting
Your Need for
Solitude

I clearly remember the day that "the mother load" overwhelmed me, and I sought refuge in our walk-in closet. I was sleep-deprived, exhausted, and surrounded by crying, needy children. My four-year-old had missed the toilet, wetting herself and the floor. My two-year-old had dumped his cereal, complete with milk. The kitchen was strewn with undone dishes from breakfast, the family room was littered with toys from the toy box, the phone was ringing, our pet birds were chirping, and the dryer was buzzing. My mind was swirling with sound, and I couldn't hear myself think. What I needed was a moment of solitude before I exploded into a thousand pieces.

And so I did the only thing I could think of: I hid in the closet.

On that particular day, it was just what I needed. Three minutes to calm my nerves, take a deep breath, reassure myself that I was a good mother (even though I *was,* at the moment, hiding from my children), and gain my composure so that I could face the rest of the day. The bad thing was that it was only 9:00 AM when I took cover.

If you're the mother of young children (or even the mother of ones now grown!), I know that you, too, have sought refuge from your children. It's okay. You can admit it. You may not have actually shut yourself in a closet, but I'm sure there have been times you've wanted to. Or maybe you've coped by imagining yourself somewhere on a sun-dappled beach, reading a book uninterrupted, a gentle breeze blowing. Or even had fantasies about returning to earlier times, known at my house as "B.C."—Before Children. Trust me, I've indulged in these same fantasies myself, sometimes simultaneously. I used to feel guilty about it, but the more I mother, the more I realize that one of a mother's greatest needs is time to rest and refuel in order to be able to keep on giving of herself.

Mothering is an intense, around-the-clock job. Being physically and emotionally available to other humans—often with no concern for your own needs—is tough work. But the tough work is made easier when we can find, or make, small pockets of time in order to reconnect with ourselves, organize our daily work, plan for the future, and communicate intimately with the God who created us.

When mothering gets difficult, my first instinct is to run and hide. I guess that's the "fight or flight" response that all humans have. My desire to flee gets greater as the noise level increases in my house, the discontent of my children heightens, or grumpiness spills from one child to the next. It kicks into high gear in the midst of a child's tantrum, when I have PMS, or when everything seems to be going wrong at the same time. It practically overwhelms me when all of the aforementioned things begin to happen at once. At my house, they often seem to.

Do you need solitude? Here are some possible indicators:

- You lose your temper more quickly and are more frustrated with your children than usual.

- You cannot think clearly.

ᜃ You're disorganized and forgetful.

ᜃ You feel disconnected from yourself, your family, and your Creator.

ᜃ You feel overwhelmed.

Although I've craved solitude almost every day since becoming a mother, I didn't discover its true power until lately. One night my kids asked me to join them in a game of Hide and Seek. I told my daughter to cover her eyes and count to ten while my son and I hid. He went to my room, and I went to his and hid in the closet. (I seem to spend a lot of time in closets, don't I?) Minutes passed. Then more minutes passed. I relaxed and started enjoying the quietness in the closet. As I sat amid the clothes and the shoes, I marveled that in my hiding spot there were no clothes to fold, no sandwiches to prepare, no school parties to organize, no appointments to keep, and no groceries to put away.

I closed my eyes and leaned back against the smooth closet wall. More minutes passed, and I used the time to reassess how I had spent my day and to make a mental "to do" list for the next day. When that was done, I began to pray, thanking God for kids and closets and the unexpected solitude I'd found.

More time passed. I couldn't imagine why my kids hadn't found me yet. Then I heard my husband's voice. "Honey, are you up here?" I whispered back, "Are the kids still looking for me?" My husband followed the sound of my voice to my son's room and entered just as I slid the closet door open a crack. When he saw me, he doubled over with laughter. "What's so funny?" I asked, feeling a bit foolish staring at him from the depths of the closet. He was laughing so hard he couldn't answer. Finally, when the laughter subsided, he confided that the kids had stopped looking for me long ago and were now involved in a game of Farm Families in our bedroom. I started to laugh, too.

But as I climbed out of my hiding spot, I realized that I had just experienced solitude in the truest sense. The dictionary defines it as "the state of being alone or remote from others; isolation." In the closet, I was truly isolated. The moments alone gave me the opportunity to be a human "being" rather than a human "doing," as I usually am. Instead of furiously working, I was "busy" sitting still.

So often in the past, my idea of solitude was simply the ability to work alone, without the "help" of a two-year-old. My "solitude" usually consisted of a long list of things I needed to accomplish, and my time alone was filled with movement and perspiration.

My minutes in the closet helped me discover that solitude is meant to be so much more than an opportunity to get things done. It is really about the beauty of silence and how it touches our soul. It is in our quiet times that we are most able to concentrate on what's important. In so doing, we are able to simplify life, regain our focus, and gather the energy necessary to continue along life's path. Now I try to practice the art of simply existing for at least five minutes a day. It's difficult. But spending time doing nothing often produces great results: ideas flow, thanksgiving wells up in my soul, peace settles in, energy is restored. And more than anything, I reconnect with the deep sense of purpose that encouraged me to become a mother in the first place.

Although my moments in the closet led me to a new understanding of the value of solitude, they weren't enough to reverse my lifelong feeling that doing means accomplishing, and accomplishing is why we're put on earth. So I'm continually relearning the value of solitude. But the lesson doesn't come easy. I feel guilty and selfish when I set aside time for myself rather than understanding that I need to rest and refuel so that I have the energy to continue to mother my kids. When I'm depleted, it's difficult to find the means to assist and respond to my children and their varied needs. But when I'm well-rested and rejuvenated, I find it much easier to embrace the fruit of the Spirit: "love, joy, peace, patience, kindness, goodness, faithfulness, gentleness, and self-control" (Galatians 5:22-23).

In her insightful book *God's Whisper in a Mother's Chaos,* Keri Wyatt Kent also acknowledges the benefits of solitude. She writes, "If I intentionally withdraw from the chaos on a regular basis, I am a more patient mother, a more loving wife and a gentler person. By spending time alone with God, I allow him to care for my soul so that I can better care for those he has entrusted to me."[1]

Jim Wallis writes in *The Soul of Politics,* "Action without reflection can easily become barren and even bitter. Without the space for self-examination and the capacity for rejuvenation, the danger of exhaustion and despair is too great."[2]

Jesus also placed importance on solitude. Several times in the New Testament we read about him "withdrawing" to a lonely place. In his book *Celebration of Discipline,* Richard Foster shows us that solitude often accompanied Jesus' work:

> He inaugurated His ministry by spending forty days alone in the desert (Matthew 4:1-11). Before He chose the twelve, He spent the entire night alone in the desert hills (Luke 6:12)....When the twelve had returned from a preaching and healing mission, Jesus instructed them, "Come away by yourselves to a lonely place..." (Mark 6:31). Following the healing of a leper Jesus "withdrew to the wilderness and prayed" (Luke 5:16). With three disciples He sought out the silence of a lonely mountain as the stage for the transfiguration (Matthew 17:1-9). As He prepared for His highest and most holy work, Jesus sought the solitude of the garden of Gethsemane (Matthew 26:36-46). One could go on, but perhaps this is sufficient to show that the

seeking out of a solitary place was a regular practice
with Jesus. So it should be for us.[3]

So it should be for us. But what of those of us who equate solitude with selfishness instead of recognizing its importance as
preparation for the tasks we have been called to do? If Jesus, who
was both God and man, needed rest, doesn't it make sense that
mothers, who are neither God nor man (but really important
women!) need rest, too? Jesus knew he needed to refuel before he
could meet the needs of the masses. As a mother, I need to rest and
refuel before I can meet the needs of *my* "mass." But how many of
us put ourselves last on the list of our "Things to Do" and are
willing to cross ourselves off the list *without* meeting our needs
when it appears we'll never make it to the end anyway?

The more we're willing to forego our own needs, including the
need for solitude, the more we're shortchanging ourselves and our
families. Solitude isn't just about being alone. It's so much more
than that.

The Benefits of Solitude

Solitude *is* about refueling. But it also provides the opportunity for us to communicate—not only with ourselves, but with
the God who created us. Not surprisingly, when we set aside time
to connect with our Creator, the Master blesses us not only by listening, but also by responding, helping us…

Gain Insight

Some of my best mothering insights have come in the midst of
solitude. And if I hadn't been quietly listening for the whisper of
God's voice, I believe I would have missed the guidance altogether.

Shortly after my daughter was born, I was up in the middle of
the night for the umpteenth time to feed and change her. Like all

mothers of newborns, I was sleep-deprived, tired, dazed, and wondering if there was somewhere I could go to return my crying daughter for one who didn't wail. At various times of the day, she would not stop crying. I paced with her. I rocked her. I cradled her in my arms and sang to her. Nothing changed her disposition. Exasperated, I laid her in her crib, turned my eyes toward heaven, and asked, "How am I ever going to make it through this?"

An answer came loud and clear in my mind: *One minute at a time.*

I breathed deeply, calmed myself, and picked up my daughter once more. I counted out 60 seconds. Then another 60 seconds. Then another. By the time three minutes had passed, Marissa was asleep in my arms, and I had a valuable new insight. *Mothering is done most effectively one minute at a time.* Though it seems like each stage of mothering will last forever, each one actually passes rather quickly. Rather than focusing on all the years of the tough task of mothering ahead, all God expects is for us to be good mothers one minute at a time. On their own, these minutes will add up into hours, days, weeks, and months. Eventually, all these millions of minutes will add up to a lifetime of good mothering. Thankfully, all I need to focus on right now is taking the parenting path one minute at a time. Knowing this keeps me from being overwhelmed.

Unbeknownst to me, my question "How am I ever going to make it through this?" was really a prayer for help. My question was actually a "listening prayer," which requires asking for guidance—and then listening to receive it. The practice often results in a clear thought or divine direction. Fellow mother and author Angela Guffey also prays listening prayers. In her book *Tender Mercy for a Mother's Soul*, she writes:

As I have learned to incorporate "listening prayer" into my spiritual disciplines, my prayer life has been severely altered. I am hearing with my heart and mind a voice that is not audible but rings in my head, making it seem louder and clearer. Some of the clear thoughts that have come to me have been very ordinary thoughts, but they seem to burn fiercely in my mind when I am listening. They include things like: *Do not turn on the television today. Call Paul and invite him to lunch. Go play with AnnaGrace.*[4]

What some might mistake for a fleeting thought, Guffey captures as God-given guidance. Her listening prayers provide the direction she needs, as do mine.

Gain Focus

Jan Johnson, author of *Living a Purpose-Full Life,* teaches us that solitude also helps us focus. As she observes, time alone helps us get to the heart of God's purpose for us. Then we can decide how to pursue that purpose in the midst of all our other responsibilities. As we work to set aside the influence of the world and to determine what God would have us do, our vision clears. Making decisions about where and how we spend our time, individually as mothers and together as a family, gets easier.

Johnson also suggests another way that solitude engenders focus—by giving us the space to find it. She writes, "We need regular solitude and getaways to establish a critical distance from our involvement. In that separate place we can ask, *Is what I do still appropriate? What needs to change?*[5] Though these two questions are important, your questions may be different. Gain focus for you and your family by using solitude to ponder the questions *you* need to answer. Here are some questions to consider:

- In what areas should I ask for help (from friends, family, spouse, pastor, teachers)?

- How is God using what's happening in my life right now to teach me?

- What's frustrating me most right now, and what can I do about it?

- What should my priorities be right now?

- Which of my own needs are not currently being met, and what can I do about it?

You may wish to record your answers to these questions in a journal. (For more on journaling, see page 23.)

In addition to providing the space necessary to wrestle with life's inevitable questions, solitude also provides the room to clean up the mental clutter that keeps us from being at peace. Author Dolores Leckey addresses this very issue. She notes:

> For all of us who desire to become more artful human beings, in touch with the creative dimensions of our family life, our work, our friendships, and in touch with the mystery of God, solitude is…an essential condition. Alone and apart, in periods of regular solitude interspersed in the daily, weekly, and monthly activities of our busy lives, we can scrape away the accretions that clutter up our interior and exterior space.[6]

It's these accretions—such as deadlines, the urgency of "To Do Lists" and undone projects—that muddy our relationships and interfere with our ability to mother more selflessly and lovingly. According to Richard Foster, "the fruit of solitude is increased sensitivity and compassion for others. There comes a new freedom to be with people. There is a new attentiveness to their needs, new responsiveness to their hurts."[7] And isn't attentiveness, ultimately, what mothering is all about?

Because the fruit of solitude is increased sensitivity and compassion for others, as a mother I have the responsibility to seek it. When I think of solitude in these terms, I no longer see it as a selfish luxury. Instead, my understanding of solitude is transformed, and I begin to view it as a necessity that will strengthen my ability to understand, encourage, and support others.

Strategies for Seeking Solitude

It's one thing to value solitude. But it's a challenge to be able to work it into a busy schedule on a regular basis. True solitude seekers know that it doesn't just happen. You have to make it happen. *But how?*

Schedule solitude just like you would any other appointment. To start, block out a brief period of time on your calendar each week, whether it's early in the morning before your family rises or in the evening after they've gone to bed. It doesn't matter when, but it does matter that you do it.

When my friend Jill and I were both home with our preschool daughters, we traded babysitting each week. Our intent was that the free time afforded each of us was to be used for something we really wanted to do. I'm not sure we stayed true to this intention, but I do know the arrangement provided us with some guaranteed solitude. Oh how I looked forward to those days…and how I miss them now that that season of mothering has passed!

If you don't have someone you feel comfortable trading babysitting with, take advantage of classes offered for preschoolers. While it may be hard to leave your child in someone else's care, it's a necessary part of the growing process. Sadly, some moms are overwhelmed with the intensity of mothering—yet they are not willing to be separate from their children even for short periods of time. While that's an admirable trait on some levels, it does increase the mothering burden and prevents kids from learning to be self-sufficient in what is usually a safe environment. Some programs require a parent to remain on the premises during activities. Our local library runs a super summer program for kids. The registration fee is only $1—but parents have to be in the library during the program. That's no problem for me. It's still an hour of solitude while my kids are listening to stories and doing crafts—and I can quietly read or write in my journal.

On occasion, when time is at a premium and my need for solitude is high, I create a comfortable "reading room" in the house with pillows and blankets on the floor. Then I invite my kids to gather an armful of books and join me for some quiet reading. They know that talking isn't allowed during this time. Sometimes I can carve out enough time for a quick Bible study with this method.

If you can afford to arrange for occasional babysitting, I highly recommend this avenue as well. At the beginning of each school year, I get a copy of the activity calendar and note the days school is not in session. A week before school holidays, I call our cadre of sitters to find one who is interested in spending a few hours with my kids while they're home. Sometimes I use the time to run errands, but often I remain on the premises while the kids are playing downstairs. I love it because I get some much-needed alone time. My kids love it because they get the undivided attention of an older friend.

I've used other strategies as well. When my children were young and my stress level was directly proportionate to the number of diapers I changed in a given day, I'd call my husband at work and let him know I needed a break. Sometimes that meant I needed one as soon as he walked in the door, and sometimes I just asked if he'd spend time with the kids after dinner so

I could take a walk around the block, make a phone call, or simply lie down for a few minutes. When things were tough, it was tremendously helpful for me to have a break to look forward to. I don't ever remember my husband saying no, and for that I'm eternally grateful. I'm not the only one who benefited. Our children did, too.

Where to Find Solitude

For a long time I thought I had to find solitude by going somewhere. It didn't seem possible that I could find it at home, so I thought I had to go to the library, or to the park, or to a bookstore. But now I'm learning that I can find it in the most unexpected places—and often at unexpected times.

More than once my kids have disappeared together into one of their bedrooms or the basement, lost in a game that only they understand. Then suddenly I have solitude! When that happens, I often have a dilemma: Should I clean house or start dinner like I had planned? Or should I take advantage of the situation and grab a book, the phone, or a few minutes at the computer? Since these moments of synergy between my children are so fleeting, I often choose the latter, knowing full well that the housekeeping will wait and that a delayed dinner won't harm anyone.

Do you have a favorite place? One you can go to when your schedule surprises you with a little free time? It doesn't have to be a room. Some women simply have a favorite chair, or a preferred spot on the sofa, or a soft blanket that can be spread on the floor. If you don't have an assigned "solitude spot," I urge you to find one. Then, when time finds you, you won't waste it deciding where to go. You'll already know.

Solitude doesn't have to occur at home. I've discovered the beauty of experiencing it in my car lately. I've started turning off the radio and enjoying the quiet. Since most mothers spend a great deal of time in the car, it's an easy place to be alone—assuming you don't have a backseat full of children!

Surprisingly, I've also discovered solitude at the grocery store. When my children were both still in diapers and hadn't started school, I often left them with my husband and grocery shopped in the evening. Granted, marketing isn't all that fun, but to me the chance to be able to shop by myself without worrying about lost pacifiers, upcoming meal times, or necessary diaper changes at inconvenient times was the closest thing I had come to heaven on earth after becoming a mother.

Since those early days, one of our grocery stores, Cub Foods, has added a "Kid Zone." Kid Zone is similar to the nursery you'd see in a church. It's a small area tucked into the corner of the store, full to the brim with toys, books, videos, and most importantly, a caring individual who is assigned to watch children while their parents shop—all at no charge! My children love it so much that they beg to go to Cub when they know it's grocery shopping day. I love it because I get to *shop alone!* I have to drive an extra 20 minutes round trip just to take advantage of this service—but it's worth it!

For those of you who are concerned about leaving your children with someone you don't know, there's a video camera that records everything that goes on in Kid Zone. And better yet, there are TV monitors throughout the store so that at any time, you can look up and make sure your kids are safe. At first I referred to the monitors often. Now, we're so comfortable with the employees in Kid Zone (thankfully, they don't change often), that I rarely need to consult the monitors for peace of mind.

Because of Kid Zone, I've been known to loiter in the produce section, meander through the meat department, and daydream in the dairy department. I spend extra time in the books and magazines section, frolic in frozen foods, and tarry in the bakery. And even though shopping is technically working, I'm doing it in solitude. I'm so spoiled by shopping alone now that when I do have to grocery shop with my children in tow, my blood pressure begins to rise before we even leave home.

If you don't have a store like this in your neighborhood, photocopy the Kid Zone information (you have my permission), highlight the information about Kid Zone, and share it with the store manager where you shop the next time you go there. Family-friendly policies make good business sense, and there's nothing wrong with making a suggestion as to how to improve your favorite grocery store.

If having a Kid Zone in your locale is a faraway fantasy, find a way to leave the kids at home—either with your spouse, a family member, a trusted friend, or a sitter. Even if you can only do this infrequently, do it. Shopping alone occasionally is well worth the effort it takes to line up child care.

If you can't find solitude at home, and finding it in the car or the grocery store doesn't appeal to you, identify other ways that meet your needs. One of my friends has an arrangement with her husband to have a "free" night every Thursday. She often goes to a bookstore, settles into a comfy lounge chair, and reads. Being surrounded by books—and mostly by silence—is as comforting for her as finding solitude in my car is for me.

Nature offers another possible source for alone time. Sometimes I'll take my kids to the park for a picnic. After we're done eating, I'll let them play on the playground equipment while I stretch out on the picnic blanket and watch them from a distance. I've also taken up running—something I never thought I'd do—simply because it is a good excuse to get out of the house. If it better suits your needs, you can slow the pace down and walk.

While you're seeking your own solitude, don't forget to share its value with your children. My friend Donna Thurston reminded me that it's important to teach our children the value of remaining quiet as well. Our kids live in a world filled with noise: Muzak in elevators; televisions in restaurants, dental offices, and minivans; and noisy video games. When Donna and her husband and two children took a two-week trip out West and visited, among other things, the Grand Canyon, she initiated "Moments of Solitude"— a few minutes dedicated to noticing the beauty of God's creation in silence. Donna noted, "When I asked the kids to be quiet and look around, they started noticing things they wouldn't normally see." She shared that her son, Tyler, became a master observer. "Mom, did you see the purple in that rock formation?" he asked after one moment of solitude. Donna hadn't. The "Moments of Solitude" helped her family share things with each other that they usually would have missed. More importantly, it gave Donna the opportunity to model the value of stillness, thereby equipping her children with a skill that will serve them well in years to come.

Seeking Solitude on Paper

Because my mind is often a chaotic jumble of random thoughts and ideas, I find it helpful to spend a portion of my solitude journaling. I don't write every day, as that goal only produced guilt in me when I missed a day and paralyzed me when I realized I just didn't have enough important stuff to work through or record on a daily basis. Consequently, I write only when I feel like it. Sometimes I'll write daily for a week, and then I won't pick up my pen for several months. But, ultimately, I come back to the blank page because that's where I'm most easily able to sort through what's happening to me, how I'm feeling, and how I'm failing. It's also where I give myself over to God and acknowledge that without him I am nothing. Journaling with his promise from Matthew 19:26 that through him, "all things are possible," is a wonderful exercise in solitude.

I'm very honest on the pages of my journal. Some days I'll simply write about what's been happening and how I feel about it. Some days I'll share an insight or spiritual breakthrough I've had. Some days I'll complain. Some days I'll compliment. I write when I'm angry and tell who I'm angry at. I write about my failures as a mother, and to keep things balanced, I also try to capture some of my successes. When I don't understand what's happening or why it's happening, I write about that, too. And I'm also sure to write about the answers to prayer that I see in my life so I have a written reminder of God's faithfulness to me. That's valuable to me as I move through the toughest days of mothering. My diary reminds me that *this too shall pass.*

Sometimes, an issue that's been floating just out of my reach will crystallize itself on the pages of my journal. Observes Julia Cameron, author of *Right to Write:*

> Just as walking aerobicizes the physical body, producing a flow of endorphins and good feelings, writing seems to alter the chemical balance of the soul itself, restoring balance and equilibrium when we are out of sorts, bringing clarity, a sense of right action, a feeling of purpose to a rudderless day. Furthermore, writing when we are out of happiness can lead us into writing from happiness.[8]

If you are honest in your journal, you will grow closer to God and come to understand him better. God will show you insights about your children and their respective needs. He'll provide clarity for you regarding your own needs, and he'll provide insights regarding the situations and issues that concern you most. Journaling is an important part of time spent alone because it is about recognition and progress. Through our writing, we recognize where we are and where we need to go. And, if we take the time, we *will* make progress.

When to Find Solitude

Another important aspect in finding solitude is not how, or where, but when. Often, as mothers, we don't get to choose when we have solitude. But for the times when we do get to plan ahead and determine when we'll have it, it makes sense to do so at the time that's best for each of us. Morning may be prime time for you. Or maybe the evening better fits your schedule. Or perhaps grabbing it in the middle of the day most fully meets your needs. Or maybe a combination of all three! Knowing in advance when you prefer to still your soul allows you to be on the lookout for opportunities that most closely meet your needs.

Since having children, I've become a morning person, which surprises me because I was never known to get up any earlier than I had to. Now I do it by choice. There's something intensely beautiful about starting the morning watching the brilliance of the sun rising. I also find that the days I can start with a few minutes to myself seem to go the smoothest. Though I used to be able to get up early and have almost an hour to myself before my mothering duties began, now I only get 10 or 20 minutes to myself—and that's if I'm lucky. But I still find it worth the effort to try and get a head start, no matter how small. That's part of the nature of solitude-seeking: As our circumstances change, so will the "how" and the "when" of how we seek aloneness.

On the days I don't get a little time to myself in the morning, I'm learning to carve a few minutes out at the end of the day. Usually I'm physically exhausted and emotionally drained, but even ten minutes spent quietly reflecting on the day pays dividends. I take time to pat myself on the back for small victories (when I didn't lose my temper but wanted to), acknowledge my shortcomings (when I *did* lose my temper and shouldn't have), and to identify the areas we need to work on as a family (like obeying the first time asked or picking up after one's self). I also commend my family into God's care so that I can sleep peacefully while he does the worrying!

Sometimes, God whispers to us. It's much easier to hear the whisper in the midst of solitude rather than trying to decipher what's being said in the midst of chaos. Give yourself the gift of solitude. Through it, you'll gain the focus and strength you need not only as a mother, but also as a child of God.

I know I need solitude. It's necessary for my health and well-being and for that of my family. As a mother, you need solitude, too.

Are you making it a priority?

Collecting Our Thoughts

- Solitude is an essential condition—and not a selfish luxury.
- Solitude results in gaining insight.
- Solitude is a means of gaining focus as to what is really important.
- The fruit of solitude is increased sensitivity and compassion for others.
- Solitude is a way to refuel so that you can continue to meet the needs of others.

For Group Discussion

1. Is solitude a luxury or a necessity for you? Why?

2. How does solitude help make you a better parent?

3. Why do you think we, as mothers, feel guilty indulging ourselves in the gift of time to ourselves?

4. What's the most effective way you've discovered to create solitude in your schedule?

5. What's your favorite way to spend your time alone?

For Personal Reflection

1. List the benefits of solitude. Which are the most important to you personally? Why?

2. Are you getting enough time alone? If not, why not?

3. If you're not getting enough time to yourself, what can you do to create more?

4. Identify one strategy for creating solitude from this chapter
   that resonated with you. Why did it appeal to you? How
   can you put it to work in your life?

What Real Live Moms Say About...
Solitude

"Sitting down and meditating, praying or taking the time to think
about things through the 'God-lens' makes it easier for me to not
overreact to things that happen. It makes things easier on me and
my family when I've poured out my fears, disappointments, and
things I'm angry about to God."

—DONNA THURSTON

"I have a big Jacuzzi tub that I fill to the brim. I either light can-
dles and soak, or I open the shades so I can see the sunrise and
hear the birds. This is a time that I use to think and meditate and
pray."

—JULIE B.

"I tend to get frustrated by the volume of things I need to deal
with, from lining up babysitters to shuttling kids to baseball practice, from taking them to doctor appointments to helping with
homework.... My alone time allows me to sort through what's in
my head and tackle it on a more manageable level. Not until I

slow down do I realize that it is often the hecticness of my pace that is overwhelming, not the tasks themselves."

—JUDY WOERNER

"My patience level is much stronger when I have time to contemplate instead of just reacting to life around me."

—TRACY COOLEY

"Driving alone in my car…can often be a time of solitude for me. This is about the only time I can listen to *my* choice of music. Music has always been an aid for me to reflect, think things through, clear and/or calm my mind, and sometimes, even pray."

—LAURA VAN PROYEN

"My solitude comes in bite-sized pieces—to and from the grocery store—and is almost never planned. If I had a plan, the kids might find out, and they would be certain to come up with something to distract me—like malaria. It's best to practice sneak attacks of solitude, whenever possible."

—DORI KNIGHT

2

Meeting
Your Need for
Friendship

Barb was my best friend in high school. We spent hours together, hanging out, talking, spending the night at each other's houses, and sharing bags of cheese popcorn in the car on the way home from school. And when our time together ended, we'd walk each other home—over and over. First, she'd walk me home. Then, because we couldn't bear to part, we'd turn around, and I'd walk her home. And then we'd repeat the cycle. Though we lived only two minutes apart, sometimes it would take us a half hour to walk each other home.

As Barb and I traced the sidewalk with our steps, walking each other back and forth and sharing our deepest hopes and fears, we created a lifelong friendship. Today, more than 20 years later, we're still confidantes. We steal time to be together when we can and e-mail between visits, knowing that though weeks, months, and sometimes even years may pass, we'll be able to pick up where we left off when the time comes. A friend like Barb is one of God's great gifts.

In the book *Celebration of Friendship*, Joy MacKenzie acknowledges our need for friendship. She writes, "Loving and being loved—being connected, valued, befriended, cherished by another—is a compelling need that permeates the life of every human being on God's earth."[1]

Though we all need to be loved, recent research suggests that women's development is more dependent on relationships than are men's. Psychiatrist Jean Baker Miller notes in her book *Toward a New Psychology of Women,* "Women's sense of self becomes very much organized around being able to make and then maintain affiliation and relationships." Men, on the other hand, place a high value on "autonomy, self-reliance, independence, self-actualization, 'listening and following' one's own unique dream, destiny and fulfillment."[2]

Women need friends. Our development depends on it. As a woman, you probably intuitively know this, even if you've never verbalized it. But sadly, when a woman becomes a mother, the first casualty is often her friendships—sometimes because of time constraints and sometimes because her new role changes her in ways that challenge her relationships. Friendships that are deep will last, while others will float away, like chaff being separated from wheat. The friendships that remain have a better chance of deepening even further, but the experience of letting some friendships go and altering others can be painful.

Our need for friendship changes throughout our lives, and friends come and go accordingly. However, the basic need for friendship does not change. Friends provide a window into our own souls. They ground us, help grow us, and hold our hand as we journey life's paths together. Women who let their friendships lie fallow during the season of mothering are more likely to feel alone. It's precisely during this time—when we're committed to raising healthy and responsible offspring—that we need the support and encouragement offered by friends.

Childhood Pals

The girlfriends who shared our childhood and teenage years powerfully influenced us. If your friends were optimistic, committed to their schoolwork, high achievers, and kind to others, you are more likely to have been so, too. If they were underachievers, constantly looking for trouble and having no respect for authority, you couldn't help but be tainted by these qualities, even if you yourself did not share them.

As Carmen Berry and Tamara Traeder, authors of *Girlfriends: Invisible Bonds, Enduring Ties*, observe, "Even if our lives take unexpected turns and we are separated by time or geography from those women who shared our childhoods, we never lose the impact that they have had on our lives. We take these girlfriends with us each and every day, in our memories as well as in the warp and weft of our personalities."[3] Indeed we do.

Our ability to forge healthy friendships is often developed during childhood. If you were able to make—and sustain—friendships in your younger days, you generally will have the confidence to do so as an adult. There are many reasons for not enjoying deep friendships as a child, however. Shyness, lack of parental support or encouragement, frequent moves, a mentally or physically ill family member, or geographic isolation are just a few of the challenges that prevent long-lasting friendships from forming. If your ability to form friendships was compromised, take heart. The ability to make friends can be developed at any stage in life.

Friendships serve many purposes, from providing companionship to aiding the development of a healthy self and worldview, from helping us navigate life's toughest moments to providing encouragement and support. Some friends are able to help us in all these areas; some are not. Some enter our lives and never leave, while others move in and out so quickly we hardly notice. All, however, have an impact.

Friendships in Motherhood

The enormous responsibility that is bestowed when a woman becomes a mother requires, by its very nature, that we make our decisions more deliberately and carefully than ever before. How we spend our time—and with whom—takes on greater significance due to the commitment we now have to our children.

Healthy friendships serve to uplift and encourage us as well as help us discover our true selves. As we share and sort through feelings with friends, we clarify our picture of who we are: conservative or liberal, introverted or extroverted, self-confident or not. Author Sue Monk Kidd summarized it this way, "We discover ourselves through our girlfriends….It's really a process, not just discovering the other person, but of discovering yourself."[4] We discover ourselves as mothers, too, as we compare notes and experiences with our friends and turn to them for guidance when necessary.

I'm learning that the roller-coaster ride of parenting is less scary when friends are along. The Bible says, "As iron sharpens iron, so one man sharpens another" (Proverbs 27:17). Mothers also sharpen one another. When we have friends to parent alongside us, not only do we benefit, but our children do as well. Being able to work through feelings often requires having someone to listen to you. And that, perhaps, is one of the greatest gifts of friendship. By talking about what's happening in our lives and how we feel about it, we're able to clarify our next steps as mothers.

In addition to helping us discover who we are, friends help us *accept* who we are, which is, perhaps, their most important function of all. With self-acceptance comes peace, clarity of purpose, and contentment. There can be none of this when an inner struggle is waging in the war of self-acceptance. It's ironic that in order to love and accept her children, a mother must first be able to love and accept herself. Consequently, achieving—and sustaining—self-acceptance is a necessary achievement for mothers, one that's aided through close friendships.

Friendship doesn't just develop us as individuals, however. It also develops us as mothers, daughters, sisters, spouses, employers, and employees. In developing us individually, it also polishes us in all the other roles we play. Our friendships, then, have the ability to strengthen (or weaken) all of our other relationships. Consequently, it's important that we carefully choose with whom we'll spend our time and energy.

Co-parenting with Friends

"Libby, it's Mary," I said into the telephone. I was a new mother, and Libby was an experienced pro as far as I was concerned, since she had two children older than mine.

"What's up?" she asked.

"It's this breast-feeding thing," I answered. "I'm spending hours each day nursing," I confided. "How can I get anything done?" I asked.

"You just don't," said Libby.

"What do you mean, 'I just don't'?" *Not meet my commitments? Heresy!* I thought.

"You just do the best you can," advised Libby.

"I seem to be nursing constantly," I complained, sensing I was about to get a life sentence. "How long will this last?" I sniveled.

"A couple of months," she answered truthfully. I knew mothering was hard work, but this was the first real indication I had that my child's need would now trump mine—from now on. But if Libby could do it, then I would, too.

This was just the first of a zillion questions Libby and my other friends have answered for me over the years. I often turn to them with questions about child-rearing. "How do you monitor your kids' TV watching?" I ask. Or, "How did you get your daughter interested in potty training?" "How do you handle it when one (or both!) of your children throws a tantrum in public?" "If your kids start playing a sport and decide they want to quit mid-season, do you let them?" The questions go on and on. And, thankfully, the answers my friends are willing to provide do, too.

The demanding nature of the mother load naturally leads women to seek each other out. Many friendships are started when women find themselves together "in the family way" or next to each other in Lamaze class. Some friendships precede pregnancy but deepen with the transition to motherhood.

Jill and I met when we sat next to each other at a business meeting before I had children. I liked her instantly, and we kept in touch by phone and an occasional lunch date. We connected on a professional level, rather than a personal level. But as we shared our joys, concerns, and disappointments in our professional lives, our friendship deepened.

One day at lunch, Jill announced she was pregnant. I was struggling with the decision about whether or not to become a parent myself, and her revelation piqued my interest. How would she handle pregnancy and maternity leave? How would she combine work and mothering? It was an opportunity for me to watch, up close and personal, how a friend navigated becoming a mother.

As it turned out, three months later, I, too, was pregnant. And rather than watching how Jill handled the transition to motherhood, I was suddenly in the boat with her, paddling alongside her. Our daughters were born six months apart, and our contact grew as we sought out each other for advice on pediatricians, babysitters, hives, and diaper rash. You name it, we talked about it.

I continue to seek out friends who are going through similar phases with their children, partly because misery loves company (just kidding!), but mostly because I know that I can learn about what's next and how to handle it from my girlfriends. And I'm not alone. When University of Wisconsin–Milwaukee sociologist Stacy Oliker asked married women what bonded them to their close friends, shared child-rearing values ranked high on the list.[5] I've noticed that shared values in regard to children have added a new depth to many of my friendships.

Because my children are two years apart, there was a period when both were in diapers, and I felt lucky just to make it to the end of a day. They commanded my entire focus and every ounce of energy I had. There were many days when I was overwhelmed with the thought that they would never grow up and I would forever be assigned to follow them around, keeping them safe and cleaning up after them.

Thankfully, a neighbor became a friend during this period. Because her children are a step ahead of mine, I've been able to watch the things she's dealing with in order to get a snapshot of what's around the corner for us. Many times, when my children have entered a new phase, I've thought to myself, *I remember hearing about this.* And somehow, the fact that she's managed to live through it is enough to get me through each stage. Now, when I'm talking to a mother with younger children, I try to reassure her of the same thing: It gets easier.

In addition to encouraging each other through the rough spots of parenthood, friends help us keep our sanity in the midst of mothering chaos. Cheryl shared this about her girlfriends, "The best thing is that just when you think your child is warped or something's going wrong or that you're a lousy parent, you talk about it in the group and somebody else laughs and says, 'Oh, I went through that,' or 'My child went through that.' It affirms the fact that parenthood is a roller-coaster ride."[6]

I remember a woman telling me about the "Barbie Mutilation" stage her son went through. For months she found her daughter's Barbies in her son's room, headless, often limbless, and even more often tied up and hanging from a doorknob. I was mortified. Wasn't this an early sign of problems down the road? I shared the story with another friend, whose mothering skills I highly respect, only to learn that her son also went through this stage. Thus, when I find the first dismembered Barbie in my son's room, I won't drag him immediately to therapy.

Practical Support

Friends provide the mental and emotional support we need as mothers—but they also provide practical support as well. I hope that you've been the beneficiary, as I have, of a home-cooked meal after the birth of your children or the blessed relief that comes when a friend calls to offer to take your children for the afternoon because she knows you're sick and need to rest. Regardless of what you think of her as a politician, Hillary Clinton was right when she boldly asserted that "it takes a village to raise a child." I've had to rely on friends more than once when I needed to be two places at one time or when I couldn't physically meet all the demands placed on me.

My family was the beneficiary of this type of support from all across the country when my almost-three-year-old niece, Skyler, was killed in a tragic automobile accident. Words cannot describe the deep sense of loss I felt—or the utter helplessness that engulfed me. I live in Illinois—my brother and sister-in-law live in Utah, where the memorial service was held. How could I be of assistance to them when I lived so far away? Friends provided the answer.

When neighbors found out, they took our kids for the afternoon—and out for dinner—so that my husband and I could grieve privately. A day later, other neighbors stopped by with dinner so that we didn't have to worry about now-mundane things like meals. Still others watched our children for the weekend, so that we could travel unencumbered to the memorial service. Yet another friend put together treat bags for my children, recognizing they were suffering the loss of a cousin. Upon our return, neighbors pitched in with meals for a week. Cards came from all over the country.

When my brother called a week after the service to accept my offer to return to Utah to help him and his wife begin the difficult adjustment to life without their daughter, another contingent of friends lined up to provide care for my children. As the weeks passed and after I returned home, friends called and e-mailed to see how we were doing. People stopped me in the grocery store, at preschool, and at church to ask about my family. Small "thinking of you" gifts arrived in the mail. The wonderful friends from my Bible-study group let me cry unabashedly in front of them—and some even cried with me.

There were so many people who helped in so many ways that I'm afraid I've missed listing someone. But you get the idea. My brother and his wife were blessed in the same way. Friends cooked for them, mowed their lawn, and watched their baby son. And friends stood by them six weeks after Skyler's death as they observed what should have been her third birthday—with a memorial tree-planting ceremony instead. Through our deep sadness we were able to see that God loves us and reaches down from heaven to gently touch us each and every day through the friends he's placed in our lives.

You don't need to experience a tragedy to see the practical help friends offer. Simply look around at the support you've received over the years, and you'll see the help of friends—and the hand of the Master Creator present and at work in your life.

Strengthening Marriage

It seems ironic that friendships with girlfriends could actually strengthen a marriage, since time spent with female friends means time spent away from one's spouse. But as close as we may be to our husbands, there are things that men just don't understand about the female experience—and the reverse is true as well. Men don't know what it is like to experience the depression and hopelessness brought on by PMS or postpartum depression; they don't have to worry about menopause or hormone replacement therapy; they don't know what it is like to birth or breast-feed a baby. And the list goes on. This lack of understanding, more than anything, is why women need friends.

A husband can't nod his head in agreement when you confide your metabolism is slowing and your nails are getting brittle. He doesn't understand the frustration you feel each holiday as you slog through all the plans and preparations alone, knowing full well that if it weren't for you, most holidays would pass unnoticed in your home. And he finds it hard to understand your sadness when you have a spat with a girlfriend. All these things, and so much more, can be discussed openly and honestly with a close female friend, as can the trials and tribulations of marriage. In fact, our friendships with women frequently help our marriages run more smoothly.

I've seen this firsthand. Often, when I've listened to friends grieve their spouse's foibles and shortcomings, I've gained a deeper appreciation for my husband's strengths. At the same time, being able to talk about my own frustrations and disappointments in my marriage has the effect of lessening them. Summarizes

Sandy Sheehy, "To a married woman, a close female friend can serve as a safety valve for everything from mild irritation to white-hot rage."[7]

Venting with a friend often keeps me from saying something in anger that should remain unsaid and helps me regain my perspective on the issue at hand. Plus, on more than one occasion, a friend has helped me realize my own shortcomings in my relationship with my husband and held me accountable for making the necessary changes in myself. I confess this isn't my favorite aspect of friendship, but I'm aware that it's an important one. I appreciate that my friends love me enough to be honest with me.

"Friends need to be able to count on each other not just for fun and affirmation, but for careful words of instruction and correction, too," writes author Annette Smith. "Committing ourselves to a friendship means that because we care on a deep, intimate level, we have the courage to speak up even when a friend needs to hear tough words of truth."[8] Surprisingly, it's this gentle guiding, when necessary, that helps strengthen my marriage, rather than detract from it.

While close friendships often support the marital relationship, there are occasions when they can become a substitute for intimacy with your spouse. Be on the alert for this. Authors Elisa Morgan and Carol Kuykendall caution that

> when we transfer a relationship of emotional intimacy from a husband to a friend, we border on the problem of committing *emotional* adultery. For the married woman, friendships are meant to complement and complete the need for intimacy, not replace it altogether so that emotional intimacy is unnecessary or neglected in the marriage relationship.[9]

If you find yourself turning to friends first or more often than your husband, be sure to check the emotional health of your marriage. It may be necessary to make a conscious decision to pursue more emotional intimacy with your husband and less with your girlfriends.

Exploring New Horizons

In addition to helping us in our relationships with our family and ourselves, friends can also get us out of our comfort zones and stretch us—and even help us conquer our fears. That's what my friend Tara did when she called to see if I'd like to take a tap dancing class with her. I had taken lessons very briefly as a child and for a semester in college, but my shoes sat in the closet gathering dust. I dug them out, called Tara back, and told her I couldn't wait to see her in *her* tap shoes.

Classes began. Our teacher, Angel, was a friendly, energetic 28-year-old who had been dancing for 25 years. She put Fred Astaire to shame! Thursday nights became special to me because I knew I got to cut loose, try new things, and have fun. Until January. That's when Angel announced it was time to start working on our recital routine.

"Recital?" I gulped. Tara hadn't mentioned anything about a recital. "Adults, too?"

"Of course," replied Angel. "You guys will steal the show!" *Only because everyone in the audience will be doubled over with laughter,* I thought to myself. But I decided to be a good sport and started working earnestly on the dance. I practiced in the kitchen while I was making dinner and practiced in the basement while my son was napping. And the closer the recital got, the more I was sure I couldn't get all the way through the dance without forgetting it and making a fool of myself. I started losing sleep over it.

As the recital drew near, Tara called to announce she had a stress fracture in her foot and wouldn't be able to perform. *A stress fracture?* I thought. *That might be a good way out for me, too!* Then I realized that I was letting the prospect of 3 minutes and 11 seconds on stage rule my life. And I decided I must do the thing that frightened me. I was going to tap dance in the recital—and I was going to do it with energy and enthusiasm. I became obsessed with overcoming what I jokingly referred to as "tapophobia"— the fear of tap dancing in public.

As I was pondering the best way to get through my fear, I recalled a piece of advice a friend had given me years before: *Act like the person you want to be.* I knew that the dancer I wanted to be would throw herself into rehearsals. So that's what I did. The dancer I wanted to be would practice outside of rehearsals. So whenever I could, I walked through the dance in order to cement it in my mind. Finally, the dancer I wanted to be would have fun being in her first dance recital at age 37—rather than dreading it. And so I began to look forward to this opportunity to do something I feared.

Dress rehearsal came. I ran into several women I knew who were accompanying their daughters to rehearsal. Several stopped me to ask if my daughter was in the recital. "No," I sheepishly answered. "I am." That's when I realized—*to my horror*—that I was the *oldest* dancer in the show. *This is crazy* I thought. *I have no business doing this!* But I knew I couldn't drop out with the recital just a day away because it wouldn't be fair to those I was dancing with. Plus, although she wasn't dancing, Tara was planning to be in the audience—my friend and my biggest fan. I knew I wouldn't be able to face her if I chickened out.

When I realized how many people I was going to know in the audience, I set my mind even more firmly. I wasn't just going to get through this recital. As they say in show business, I was going to "sell it." And I did. (For the record, I made one small mistake but I kept right on dancing and smiling, and I don't think people noticed. If they did, they were too polite to mention it.)

And so, at age 37, I conquered "tapophobia" and have since danced in two more recitals. And I did it by acting like the person I wanted to be—thanks to sage advice and encouragement from my friends. Had it not been for Tara, I never would have added this experience to my life. Nor would I have learned firsthand that the best way to conquer fear is to go right through it.

Modeling Friendship

In addition to stretching us, I believe our personal friendships play another important role in our lives: They introduce our children to the high value that should be placed on a relationship with another human being. My parents' own friends played a large role in my upbringing. I still love to read their Christmas cards to my mom each year to find out what's going on with their families and to reconnect with those who helped shape who I am today.

I remember as a child going camping with my parents and their friends. And listening to them as they played cards at our house. And watching the outpouring of love when they showed up for a surprise birthday party for my mom. Friends have been such an integral part of my parents' lives that it's only natural that my own friends would become an important part of mine.

Because I've been blessed through my friendships, I desperately hope and pray that my children will also be blessed in this way. I pray that God will bring Christian friends into their lives. I also pray that he'll help my children learn to be good friends, and that, when necessary, they'll learn how to let go of friends who are leading them astray. We shouldn't underestimate the importance of modeling healthy friendships for our children because when our children clearly see the value we place on friendships, they will be more likely to place a high value on them as well.

Letting Go

Most of us spend more time and energy making friends than we do letting them go. But it would be shortsighted to discuss the importance of friendship without also addressing the need to gently end a friendship when it becomes necessary. It wasn't until my early twenties that I had to consciously make the decision to end a friendship. It was painful. And it was the first time I realized that healthy friendships require a balance of give and take, of closeness and distance, of walking alongside one another rather than one person carrying the other. Healthy friendships offer advice and encouragement; they are not bossy. They offer practical support, and no offense is taken when the support is not accepted. They provide a sounding board and confessional; they do not pass judgment. And above all, they can survive the ebb and flow of life.

Though I believe God often puts us in unbalanced friendships so that we might do some good, I don't believe he expects us to stay in them at the expense of our own emotional or physical health. As mothers, the demands on our time and emotions are already so great that we have to be especially diligent not to entertain any friendships that drain our energies, drag us down, or burden us unnecessarily. Author Gordon MacDonald offers practical advice to help determine the types of friendships we should seek. He writes:

> I can think of certain people in my world whose company invigorates me, and when they leave, I am full of resolve, ideas, and intentions about God, self-improvement, and service to others. I can also think of people in my world whose presence exhausts me. And when they leave, I am ready for a long, long nap.[10]

It's those who invigorate us who should be most sought after as friends. Those who exhaust us should be avoided. Some people are tiring because they are happier when they are unhappy. Others are crisis junkies, needing to always be in the midst of crisis, from which they gain their self-worth. Still others are masters at tearing people down in order to build themselves up. Angela Guffey writes about a friend like this, along with her resulting wake-up call:

> Many years ago, there was a woman in my life who had decided that she was going to be my friend. She was a sweet person who loved the Lord, but we lacked a real soul connection. This woman called me almost every day, and because I was lonely at home with my first baby, I began to embrace her as a friend. Never mind that her attitude was dismal and depressing. Never mind that our theologies took divergent paths. Never mind that she was miserable in her marriage and in life. Never mind that her walk with the Lord was shallow and sporadic.
>
> …I finally woke up that day and realized that this friendship was not healthy for me. This woman could be in my life, but I would not give her permission to walk around in my soul.[11]

I would not give her permission to walk around in my soul. That's the key. We must guard our hearts and not give permission for just anyone to walk around inside us. That's sacred ground, and it must be preserved for those who encourage and uplift us as well as challenge us to become better in all the roles we play.

Sometimes the death of a friendship is attributable to circumstances beyond our control: a change in economic status that stresses the friendship, the stark reality of differing values or opinions, or a turbulent time that can't be navigated successfully together. Easing out of a friendship is easiest if both individuals realize the necessity of moving on. It's most difficult when only one person wants to end the friendship. Sometimes relationships die simply from neglect. Others require a deliberate effort to "break up" with the friend. Both types of endings can be painful.

I've tried to be gracious about the deaths of the friendships I've endured. It's not easy. In some cases, ill-will remains despite my best efforts to move on. If this happens to you, go to God and ask him to transform your negative feelings into thankfulness that the relationship ever existed. It's also helpful to identify how the relationship benefited you so that the time you spent as friends doesn't seem wasted. Most importantly, learn from each loss so that you have even more to offer your friendships in the future.

The Best Friend of All

If you've ever doubted your need for close friends, you need look no further than the Bible. Though Jesus selected 12 men for the practical purpose of continuing his ministry after his death, three made up Christ's inner circle: Peter, James, and John. It was these three who accompanied Jesus when he raised Jairus' daughter from the dead (Mark 5:35-37), who witnessed Jesus' glory on the Mount of Transfiguration (Matthew 17:1-2), and perhaps most telling of all, who were invited to join Jesus as he prayed in anguish at Gethsemane the night before his death (Mark 14:32-34).[12] In his darkest hour, even Jesus turned to friends for support. That's a strong testament to the value of friendship.

I was blessed to grow up in a Christian home. But as a child, I only knew Jesus as Lord, Jesus as the Son of God, and Jesus as Savior. I had never thought of him as my friend. Then, one Sunday morning when I was 14 and uncertain about my value as a person, questioning God and doubting everything about my young life, I was introduced to the hymn "What a Friend We Have in Jesus."

*What a friend we have in Jesus, all our sins and griefs to
 bear!*
What a privilege to carry everything to God in prayer!
*O what peace we often forfeit, O what needless pain we
 bear,*
All because we do not carry, everything to God in prayer.

*Have we trials and temptations? Is there trouble any-
 where?*
*We should never be discouraged; take it to the Lord in
 prayer!*
*Can we find a friend so faithful who will all our sorrows
 share?*
*Jesus knows our every weakness; take it to the Lord in
 prayer!*

*Are we weak and heavy laden, cumbered with a load of
 care?*
*Precious Savior, still our refuge—take it to the Lord in
 prayer!*
*Do thy friends despise, forsake thee? Take it to the Lord
 in prayer!*
*In his arms he'll take and shield thee; thou wilt find a
 solace there.*[13]

As I sang the words above, I realized, for the first time, that in addition to being my Creator, Lord, and Savior, Jesus was also my Friend. I am especially touched by the idea that we forfeit peace and bear needless pain when we don't share our burdens with Christ. Now I know that Jesus listens to my disappointments, heals my hurts, helps celebrate my successes, and when I fail, he gently scoops me up in his arms and says, "I am here with you. Let's try it again." What comfort it is to know that even when my earthly friends don't understand or can't walk with me, Jesus will!

While it's true that mothers need earthly friends, in this season of life it's especially important not to forget your friendship with Jesus, the best friend of all.

Let's Get Together!

It's rare that friendship "just happens." Friendships must be fed and nurtured in order to grow. The following ideas will help if you're seeking new friends or looking for ways to grow your current friendships.

- Create a connection between the moms in your neighborhood by inviting them, with their children, over to your house (or to a local park) for an informal gathering. Keep refreshments simple. I did this in my neighborhood, and we enjoyed it so much it became a regular event, with different moms hosting each month and all of us pitching in to help with food and drinks.

- Organize a group trip to an indoor play area or something similar. Everyone pays their own way, and friends can come and go as their schedule permits. Every time I do this, I always hear the words, "We should do this more often!"

- For many years my friend Donna hosted a "Christmas Tea" for her daughter's friends and their mothers. The tea featured a visit from Mrs. Claus and a small gift for each child. More importantly, it offered the opportunity for mothers and their daughters to spend time together. A similar activity can easily be created for mothers and sons or fathers and sons.

- Every other month, I meet with a group of seven friends for "Cooking Light Night." We gather for the sole purpose of learning how to cook healthier together. One person is in charge of hosting the event (we rotate homes), and another is in charge of planning the menu and assigning a dish to each person in the group. Those assigned dishes familiarize themselves with the recipe, bring the necessary ingredients, and show how the recipe is prepared when their turn comes during our cooking fest. The best part of the evening is sitting down to eat the meal we've prepared together and enjoying the fellowship that occurs.

↬ Check your local paper for organized groups meeting in your area. Our paper recently announced a meeting for gardeners and the formation of a new book club.

↬ One of my sisters-in-law meets regularly with a quilting group, and together they've created some beautiful stitched works. Other women I know meet to scrapbook or do crafts together. The types of groups that can be formed are limited only by your imagination!

↬ Host an earring party. Attendees are asked to bring five pairs of earrings they no longer wear, each pair wrapped individually. Attendees sit in a circle with the earrings in the middle. Guests take turns rolling a pair of dice and a seven, eleven, or doubles wins the chance to pick one of the packages. When guests begin to roll a second time, a seven, eleven, or doubles wins the right to either pick another package from the pile of earrings in the middle or to take an unwrapped package from another participant. After all the packages are distributed, everyone opens their "new" earrings. You'll hear lots of laughter, stories about the origin of some of the earrings, and "oohs" and "aahs" from those who got earrings they like. At this point, guests can exchange the earrings they won't wear for ones they will. Any leftover earrings can be donated to a women's shelter.

↬ In 1990, authors Kathleen Laing and Elizabeth Butterfield launched an annual adventure they call the "Sisters Weekend." In their book *Girlfriends' Getaway*, they write about their first year. "We spent a weekend together crowded into a single hotel room—all six of us! The space was tight, and we tripped over each other. But we left for home at the end of our first getaway already making plans for the following year. We haven't missed a getaway since."

It's not just the getting away that's important though—it's what happens when you're away, as Laing and Butterfield share: "We've laughed, hugged, prayed, and cried together. We've supported each other through crises, losses, and heartaches. But mostly it's been a blessing just to get away from the stresses."[14] And, don't forget, a chance to get away from diapers…and the dishes…and the laundry… and so on.

Several years ago, my friend Pam invited *all* of her friends to join her at her parents' vacation home. Of those invited, two friends were able to join her (I was one of them) for a long weekend of relaxing by the pool, talking, and enjoying the sun. I treasure the memories from that trip.

When Kim Newlen left her teaching job to stay home with her daughter, she experienced loneliness. Instead of wallowing in it, she decided to do something about it. She created a monthly gathering for women that didn't require an RSVP or the need to extend a reciprocal invitation. The gatherings, called "Sweet Monday®," offer brief spiritual encouragement, dessert and candy to match the theme, and most importantly, fun! Now, almost ten years after the first group met, Sweet Monday is providing even more opportunities for fellowship as women across the country have adapted the idea. Kim, the lonely mom, has now turned into an encourager extraordinaire and has written *Sweet Monday, Women's Socials on a Shoestring Tied to a Generous God.* (You can learn more about Sweet Monday at www.sweetmonday.com.)[15]

Mothers Need Friends

It's tempting to put friendships on hold as we struggle to meet the changing needs of our families and attempt to keep up with all that is demanded of us as mothers. But mothers need friends. Not just *any* friends, but pals we can walk alongside and bare our souls to. Friends who encourage and applaud us. Friends who will catch us when we stumble, dry our tears when necessary, and send us on our way again with love and encouragement.

Though motherhood forces us to make tough choices about who we'll spend our time with, and how much time we can afford to spend nurturing our friendships, it's important that we don't limit our friendships only to other mothers. To do so would be a mistake. Diversity in our friendships strengthens us by making us well-rounded and more open-minded. I have friends that think like me and friends that don't. I have single friends and married friends. I have friends much older and many younger. I also have friends of varying ethnic and religious backgrounds. I'm drawn to each of them for a different reason. Together, this diverse group of friends creates a beautiful tapestry of community. I believe that God has placed each one of these people in my life for a different purpose. Some will be in my life for a short season; some are present for a specific reason. Some are to help mature me, and some are to teach me to lighten up. All are helping me become the woman God created me to be.

Mothering is intense work, but it's made more pleasant when joy and sadness can be shared with a trusted friend—including Jesus, the best Friend of all.

Collecting Our Thoughts

- Women need friends.

- Healthy friendships help sharpen us in all the roles we play: mothers, wives, employers, employees, and so forth.

- Due to the demands on our time as mothers, friendships must be carefully selected.

- The parenting journey is more fun and less scary when it is shared with friends.

- Friends offer practical support...sometimes at the most unexpected times.

- Friends encourage us to try new things and conquer our fears.

- Sometimes it's necessary to let a friendship go.

- Jesus is the best friend of all.

For Group Discussion

1. How have your friendships with other women changed since becoming a mother?

2. Is seeking and/or maintaining friendships a priority in your life? Why?

3. Do you believe your friendships enhance your role as a mother? How so?

4. What's the most fun or creative thing you've done with a friend(s) to keep the ember of friendship glowing?

5. Proverbs 27:17 says, "As iron sharpens iron, so one man sharpens another." How do your friendships sharpen or dull you?

For Personal Reflection

1. Name some of your closest friends throughout the years. Identify how each of these friendships has benefited you.

2. Is there a friendship in your life that's currently lying fallow? If it's one you'd like to rekindle, spend a few minutes making plans to reconnect.

3. Are you putting too much, just enough, or not enough priority on your friendships right now? If you answered too much or not enough, list several steps you can take over the next two weeks to either reconnect with your friends or rebalance the priority between your friends and family.

4. Is there a friend in your life right now who isn't a good influence on you or your family? If so, what adjustments do you need to make in this friendship?

What Real Live Moms Say About...
Friendship

"Hearing how friends handle situations gives me new ideas, and just knowing someone else has struggled as I do sometimes lets me know I'm not alone."

—LORI H.

"During the busy season of Christmas, I have a friend who gets in the car with me, and we run errands together. We also have done lots of shopping around and helping each other with opinions on furniture."

—BETH S.

"One of my friends is great at sneaking little gifts onto my front porch."

—AMY KENNEDY

"When I was pregnant with my youngest child, it was discovered that she had a severe heart defect that would eventually result in open-heart surgery. I had to go to the doctor several times a week, and oftentimes I wouldn't be able to pick my daughter up from school. My friend would pick my daughter up, and sometimes even keep her overnight so that my husband and I could have some time together."

—CHONDRA WILLIAMS

"A while back, my closest friend and I had an overnight getaway. We didn't leave town, but we got a hotel room that had a Jacuzzi in it. We brought some stuff and created our own little spa getaway. We highlighted each other's hair and gave ourselves manicures and facials. We ordered a pizza and sat up chatting most of the night—just like we did together back when we were thirteen."

—LORI MCCLURE

"I schedule [time with a friend] on my calendar just as if it were an appointment. For example, every Thursday morning I have coffee with my best girlfriend. When our children were small, we met at one another's home and brought the children along."

—DEVONNE WHITE

3

Meeting
Your Need for
Balance

Is there really such a thing as balance in our modern, over-worked, fast-paced world? I wonder. We're inundated with choices, overwhelmed with conveniences that previous genera-tions never even imagined, and subjected to more demands on our time than ever before. The decisions we have to make each day continually increase. In 1978, there were 11,767 items in the average grocery store; today the number is over 24,500 (including more than 186 types of breakfast cereal!). Satellite dishes routinely bring us a choice of more than 1,500 movies every month.[1] Cars have more options than ever before. The range of children's activ-ities has burgeoned in the last two decades. Organized soccer didn't even exist during my childhood, and there certainly weren't competitive hockey or gymnastics teams!

In addition to option overload, we're suffering from informa-tion overload. Round-the-clock news coverage and automatic e-mails keep us apprised of what's going on all over the world. (Did you know that the average person spends more than eight years of his or her life watching TV?)[2] For those who prefer to get their news from a paper, there are more than 1,700 daily newspapers to choose from throughout the country.[3] And if you read only one edition of the Sunday *New York Times,* you'll get more information than a typical adult in 1892 was exposed to during his entire life![4] Throw in the fact that more than 40,000 new books are published in this country every year, and it's easy to see why we're drowning in data.[5]

We're not just faced with more choices though—we have less time to make them. The average working American puts in 163 more hours per year than they did 20 years ago. Men are working an average of 2½ weeks longer per year, women 7½ weeks longer than in the 70s.[6] (Is the inequity any surprise?) The time squeeze doesn't only affect adults. Children today have 75 percent of their weekday programmed, up from 60 percent in 1981.[7]

As a result of all this, many of us are sleeping less. Though the average adult needs eight hours of sleep each night, nearly one in three Americans sleep as little as six hours or less per night during the workweek. Children are affected, too; many are getting one to two hours *less* sleep than they need each night.[8] The result? Drowsy, grumpy people. Slowly we're turning into a nation of busy, sleep-deprived individuals.

Is it any wonder we have to work so hard just to keep up?

Though the Bible was written long before the days of kids' soccer, T-ball, organized football, and cheerleading clinics for first graders, it has something to say about balance—more succinctly and more poetically than I ever could. Think about the wisdom in the words of Ecclesiastes 3:1-8:

> There is a time for everything, and a season for every activity under heaven:
>
>> a time to be born and a time to die,
>> a time to plant and a time to uproot,
>> a time to kill and a time to heal,

a time to tear down and a time to build,
a time to weep and a time to laugh,
a time to mourn and a time to dance,
a time to scatter stones and a time to gather them,
a time to embrace and a time to refrain,
a time to search and a time to give up,
a time to keep and a time to throw away,
a time to tear and a time to mend,
a time to be silent and a time to speak,
a time to love and a time to hate,
a time for war and a time for peace.

There is a time for everything. Understanding this at a gut level is the key to achieving balance in today's crazy world and to keeping sane as you manage the mother load.

According to the *American Heritage Dictionary*, balance is "the power or means to decide." Doesn't the idea of achieving balance take on new meaning when you realize it means exercising the power to decide (as opposed to trying to get the arms on a balance scale to hang perfectly even)?

My informal observations tell me that as mothers we often believe we've lost the power to decide as a result of all the choices now available. We've allowed ourselves to become slaves to our children's school schedules, their sports schedules, their dance schedules, and their music lessons schedules. And though it is true that once we've allowed our children to commit to any of these activities, we have an obligation to follow through, it's also true that we have the ability—and the obligation—to ask ourselves what's most important at any given time. We have the power to decide when someone (namely us) needs to step in and call a halt to the insanity of today's overloaded schedules. We are *not* powerless in this regard.

In the midst of the wild racing about we all do, we have a duty to teach our children about the importance of setting and keeping priorities. If they don't learn it from us, chances are they won't learn it. How sad it would be if we raised a generation of children who felt overwhelmed and pulled in multiple directions and tried to be all things to all people, only to discover the emptiness that comes with this lack of focus. Instead, we can show the importance of setting priorities...and making wise choices based on these priorities. Modeling this type of harmony is a phenomenal gift to our children and to the future generation(s) they will one day influence.

As we exercise this power, our goal should be to create an overall evenness in our lives. If you have a week of frenzied activity in your home, you should also have a period of calm. If you have a lot of going out, you should have some staying home. If you have serious study, it should be balanced with play and laughter. Though there never will be an equal amount of play and work, going out and coming in, and laughter and tears, if we focus on making sure we have some of each of these things in our lives, then we are balanced.

There is no one perfect way to achieve this "evenness" in life. However, we can create it by using a variety of techniques together. Some of what follows are my own techniques, others have been gathered from people much wiser than I. Some ideas are easier to implement than others. All are designed to help create harmony. I urge you to select the methods that speak most directly to your heart—and to begin using them immediately. You'll be surprised at how quickly you'll see results.

Know Your Priorities

The most important aspect of creating symmetry in your life is knowing your priorities. This may sound rather simple, but our priorities often get buried under piles of laundry, forgotten in the midst of deadlines, or thrown out with the McDonald's Happy Meal bags as we race from commitment to commitment. If you know your priorities, it's much easier to determine how you'll spend your time.

I can sum up my priorities in one phrase: To raise healthy, happy, and responsible children. Everything in my life right now stems from that. (I'll admit this is rather simplified because it doesn't address my relationships with God, my husband, or other family members, all of which are important. But, at this point, as I'm pulled in many directions, I believe the simpler my priorities, the better. For decision-making purposes, I've summed them up in one phrase, even though I know life is more complicated.) My "priority phrase," as I call it, provides a method by which to determine where and how I should be spending my time during this period of my life.

As I write this, my church is in the process of expanding its staff by adding an associate pastor. Part of this individual's job will be focused on working with the youth of our congregation. Because I know this person will be interacting with my children, and that finding the right person will help me in my quest to raise "healthy, happy and responsible children," I said yes when I was asked to serve on the search committee. But I've turned down other requests, both from inside and outside the church, because they wouldn't help me meet my stated priority at this time.

Setting priorities does not mean that you'll never get to do anything *you* want to do just for yourself. It simply offers a means by which to measure the value of an activity *at this time* and *in relation to what's important to you*. It doesn't mean you have to say no to everything that doesn't perfectly fit into your list of priorities. But if you want to say no to something, being able to justify it in your own mind before uttering the word "no" makes it easier.

As we discuss priorities, let me note that these will (and should) change throughout your life. My priorities now, as a mother, can't be, nor should they be, the same as they were when I was childless in my twenties. Priorities need to be revisited—and reworked—on a regular basis.

Each December for the past several years, I've set aside time to reevaluate my priorities and set goals for the year ahead. It's amazing how writing these down helps manifest what I want to happen in my life. At the top of the page, I write out Proverbs 16:9: "In his heart a man plans his course, but the Lord determines his steps." Then, after prayerful brainstorming, I cast a vision for myself for the upcoming year, followed by four or five objectives covering the things I want to do or the areas in my life I want to work on. The exercise fits into a morning, and the results of my work never take up more than two sheets of paper, which I post on the wall near my computer.

If your reaction to this idea is that it's too organized, too formal, or simply impossible due to the stage of mothering you're in, please reconsider. I, too, used to think this was a futile way for a mother of young children to spend her time. *Who has time to focus on anything other than the children?* I thought. And then, because I was desperate to gain some clarity and focus in my life, I tried it. And I've been doing it ever since. The exercise helps me focus on what's important for the year ahead, as well as providing an opportunity to review the surprises and blessings of the year just past. Finally, and perhaps most importantly, it gives me a feeling of control, which is lacking in other areas of my life right now due to the young ages of my children.

If formal goal-setting doesn't appeal to you, you might consider an idea from author Leslie Charles. Each year, she selects an annual theme. She started this idea in 1995, when she felt a professional growth spurt coming on. Leslie chose "The Year of Transition" as her theme, imagining that she was moving to a new level, personally and professionally. Her themes come to her sometime in the last quarter of the year. A word often just pops up in conversation and if it resonates with her, she takes it as her theme for the year.[9]

I adopted this idea in 2001, beginning with "The Year of Surprise," during which I wanted to be surprised by God working in my life. I wasn't disappointed. Since then, I've also observed "The Year of Anticipation" (during which I anticipated the work God would do through me), "The Year of Courage" (during which I hoped to be brave enough to start pursuing some long-suppressed dreams), and "The Year of Fluidness" (during which I planned to be more flexible and go with the flow, rather than trying to control life and make things happen). Having the laser focus offered by my annual theme and my goals and objectives has made it easier for me to maintain evenness in my life. It will do the same for you, too. No longer am I pulled from one activity to the next without purpose. Now there's a reason for everything I do.

Know Your Capacity

Another necessity for creating balance in your life is knowing your capacity. When boating on a river in Illinois, I noticed a line painted around the barges, near the point where the vessel rested in the water. Curious, I asked what it was for and learned that the line is a guide for loading the boats. If too much is loaded, the line disappears beneath the water and the boat is in danger of sinking. If the line rests too high above the water, it's an indication that the boat isn't carrying as much as it was designed to hold. Each barge is designed to carry a specific amount.

There's a lesson here for us as well. Knowing our personal capacity is important so that we don't overload ourselves—or skim through life without realizing our full potential. We were made by our Creator for a specific purpose and to carry "just the right amount." When I was younger, I used to compare myself to other people. I'd look around and see women who seemed to be managing all their commitments with no difficulty. Women who were juggling new stepfamilies, children of their own, full-time jobs, and an attempt to get a master's degree on top of all that. I'd wonder to myself, *How do they do it?* and then proceed to feel guilty because I wasn't doing—and probably couldn't do—the same.

On the surface, these women's boats seemed seaworthy. But what I couldn't see was the part of the boat that was underwater. Was it *truly* seaworthy? Or were there a few leaks here and there? What I couldn't see was how these women really were handling the pressure of their multiple commitments. Were they short-tempered with their families? Were they happy? Or miserable? Did they fall into bed exhausted each night? Were they up doing laundry and packing lunches at five o'clock in the morning? Some ships can function like that. I can't. Being able to identify—and admit to—our limitations doesn't come easily. But it is essential if we're going to find balance in our lives. It's necessary to know our capacity so that we can keep our painted line above the water. Staying afloat is necessary for our health and happiness, and for that of our families.

It's also essential that we avoid falling into the comparison trap. That's when we start listening to all the activities our friends and neighbors are involved in—and feeling guilty because little Johnny isn't playing baseball *and* soccer *and* on the swim team, too. Or feeling panicked that Sarah hasn't started piano lessons like everyone else her age. The comparison trap is dangerous because it encourages us to do things because everyone else is, not because it's best for our family or because the time is right.

You can avoid the dangers of the comparison trap by following this advice: *Act on what you know.* Isaiah 42:20 addresses this very issue. It says, "You have seen many things, but have paid no attention; your ears are open, but you hear nothing." Balance requires seeing and hearing—and therefore *knowing*—what's best for your family. Trust your judgment. You know what's best better than anyone.

I have a friend who provides activities for her children from the time school is out for the summer until the time it starts again in the fall. I used to feel guilty that our summer schedule didn't look the same. But *what I know* about my family is that my kids are happiest and most cooperative when the majority of their time is unscheduled. Consequently, it would be a mistake if I tried to replicate my friend's schedule.

Your schedule in your house should be determined by what you know about each of your family members, not influenced by what everyone else seems to be doing. By acting on what you know, you can reduce guilt and create schedules and routines that work for *your* family, rather than making decisions that are better for someone else's family. It sounds simple, but acting on what you know is really a profound piece of wisdom. Practice doing it for a week and see what happens.

Let Go

It's not physically possible to keep adding to your list of activities and responsibilities week in and week out and be able to continue to meet your commitments. With more and more to do, yet no more time to do it in, at some point you'll reach the point of paralysis (or a breakdown!) and won't be able to do anything at all.

To avoid getting to this point, when considering a new activity ask yourself, "What can I let go of to make room for this new obligation?" Then, make deliberate plans to drop an activity in order to be able to add the new one. With discipline like this, you'll rarely be out of balance. If, however, acting with such careful discipline doesn't come easily to you and you find yourself off-kilter, practice the art of winnowing. To winnow means "to examine closely in order to separate the good from the bad." That's really what balance is: deciding what's most important and acting on it.

As author Gordon MacDonald notes, balance means choosing the best of the good. He writes, "Years ago my father wisely shared with me that one of the great tests of human character is found in making critical choices of selection and rejection amidst all of the opportunities that lurk in life's path. 'Your challenge,' he told me, 'will not be in separating out the good from the bad, but in grabbing the best out of all the possible good.'"[10] Separating the best out of all the possible good can be a challenge, but one that's necessary in our search for balance.

Winnowing, or narrowing the number of things on your "to do" list, requires consciously identifying the activities that you can forego doing. Some will drop off your list forever (You don't really want to finish the cross-stitching you started as a senior in high school, do you?), and some will simply be postponed (maybe even until the kids are out of the house!). The key is having the courage to move an activity off your radar screen so it no longer hangs over your head or makes you feel guilty. Some of these may be activities that you've been involved in for years.

If you haven't closely examined your schedule recently, it may be time to take a hard look at it and let go of activities that are no longer top priorities. It might also require eliminating some of your children's activities for the benefit of your family. But that's the goal of winnowing: Identifying the best activities for your family *at this time*, based on *what you know*.

Learn to Say No

Do you find it difficult to say no—even to things you're not interested in? I can't begin to tell you the number of times I've said yes out of a feeling of obligation, fear of hurting someone's feelings, or because I thought I should. The arrival of my children has actually made it easier to say no since I now have a wonderful reason *not* to be overcommitted outside our home. But I also have more things to say no to since the kids have a myriad of activities to choose from and I have more groups looking for help as a result. In light of this, mastering the art of saying no makes it easier to stay in balance.

The ability to say no is actually a process that begins long before you're asked to do something. As discussed earlier, when your priorities are in order, it's easier to determine which activities should end up on your schedule and which shouldn't. When you're clear about your priorities, you'll be more clear about when to say yes and when to say no.

If you're one of the many women who have difficulty saying no, it's helpful to recognize *that saying yes to something means you're also indirectly saying no to something else.* In other words, when you agree to be homeroom mother for your daughter's class, you're committing a chunk of your time—and losing the ability to use it for something else. *Whatever you say yes to in life takes time away from something else you could be doing, so consider your "yeses" carefully.*

To keep from overcommitting, here's a question to ask whenever you're asked to do something: "May I think about it and get back with you?" Doing so gives you the opportunity to weigh the cost of any yes in your life before you commit. Find out how much time the project will take, survey your calendar for the upcoming weeks and months, and ask yourself, "What would saying yes to this also mean saying no to?" It's easier to say no if you know the cost of your yes first.

Learn to Say No Without *Saying No*

For those of you that have trouble using the word "no," learning how to say it without actually saying the word is a valuable skill. For some reason, not having to use the word actually makes it easier to turn down an opportunity. Here's an example. Let's say you've been asked to chair a fund-raiser at your child's school. And let's also say you're not interested, but you don't want to hurt anyone's feelings and you want to preserve your relationship with the person who is asking. Try this: "I appreciate your confidence in me, but I don't want to make a commitment I can't keep." As you can see, the word no does not appear anywhere in this sentence. However, you just said no, kindly and politely.

Another good phrase is: "I'm flattered to be asked, but this isn't the best time for me to be involved." Suggesting someone else for the task is another gracious way to say no without *really* saying it. I like this approach: "As much as I'd like to help, I'm not gifted artistically. How about calling Beth Hahn or Betsy Winthrop?" (Granted, Beth and Betsy may not be happy with you, but you've actually complimented them by offering their names for consideration!) Here are some other ways to say no without using the word:

- ✍ "I limit the number of volunteer activities I do each year, and I'm already at my limit. Thanks for asking, though."

- ✍ "I'm working on a rather large project right now that prevents me from getting involved. I appreciate the work you're doing, however."

- "Thank you for asking me to_____. I'm sorry I won't be able to, but I appreciate being asked."
- "I'm not available at this time."
- "My available time and resources are already committed. But thanks for asking."
- "I've already got plans." (Those plans might be to spend some time alone or *not* to go someplace that requires spending money. Both are legitimate and should be honored.)

If you don't want to say no, but you aren't interested in doing what you've been asked, negotiate or make a counteroffer. Ways to negotiate or counteroffer include asking:

- "Would you mind if I asked someone to co-chair this activity?"
- "Is there something else I could do to help that would take less time?"
- "Although I'm unable to do this myself, would it be helpful if I made a couple of calls and found someone else to do it?"

Mastering these phrases and questions will make it easier to keep your life in balance—without ever having to use the word "no." When used in conjunction with the other tips in this chapter, these phrases pack a powerful punch. And the key in negotiating is knowing what you are willing to do, and then asking for the opportunity to do it.

But what if there are things you're currently doing because there's no one else to do them? If you've been guilted into doing something because of this, let me give you a few things to think about.

First, if there's no one else to do it, perhaps it should not be done at all. *Gulp!* I know those are tough words to think about, but if you find you're doing things because no one else wants to, you need to ask yourself if they really are important. Peter F. Drucker, a renowned consultant, says, "There is surely nothing quite so useless as doing with great efficiency what should not be done at all." What a profound thought!

Sister, the world is changing rapidly and "we've always done it this way" or "our church has been doing this for 50 years" are not good enough reasons to continue doing something. I'm not saying you shouldn't do things because no one else wants to, but I am suggesting that you carefully and thoughtfully make a deliberate decision about those things. Maybe it is time to start a new tradition or end an old one.

Here's another important thought: Maybe there's no one else to do it because *you're* doing it! Why expect someone else to step forward to volunteer to do something that's already being capably done? Sometimes, in order to find a new volunteer, you have to let an activity or program lapse. When it is missed, someone will step forward to breathe new life into it. If it isn't missed, then perhaps it was past its prime and time to be retired anyway.

If you're doing something you don't enjoy or aren't good at simply because there's no one else to do it, have the courage to submit your resignation—with plenty of notice—and then step away from the project according to the deadline you've set. If the program has value, a replacement for you will be found. If a replacement isn't forthcoming, a new activity will spring up in its place—one that can attract the volunteers necessary to run it.

While your sense of duty may make it difficult for you to bring your involvement to an end, I can attest that the world will not stop spinning as a result. It's much healthier to be involved with something because you're passionate about it or because you enjoy doing it rather than being active because there is no one else to do it. (Please note that I'm not suggesting that you never take on an assignment that you don't want to do. We all have to do things we don't enjoy, but these should comprise only a small part of our total time commitment. The majority of activities we're involved with should be ones we enjoy and/or are good at.)

Establish Policies

Another way to say no without having to speak the word is to establish policies, an idea shared by Mary LoVerde in her book *Stop Screaming at the Microwave.* She writes, "[Businesses] are not singling out any individual. They have thought long and hard about how to run their company and apply their policies across the board. There are return policies, investment policies, and insurance policies—in fact, most of what they do is influenced by a policy." Mary suggests developing policies similar to those developed by businesses to help manage your family's affairs. (In fact, by definition, policy means "wisdom in the management of affairs.") In a survey Mary conducted for her book, she asked respondents to share samples of their personal policies. Here's what they wrote:

- ᖇ We do not discuss bad behavior or problems at dinner.
- ᖇ We don't write checks on Sunday.
- ᖇ The car doesn't move until everyone is buckled up.
- ᖇ Half of all allowance money every week goes into savings.
- ᖇ We always light a candle at dinner to add to our quiet talking and eating time.
- ᖇ No one is allowed to say "shut up."

- I say no to any commitment that takes me away from my children in the summer.

- Thursday is Mom's night out.

- We always say grace, even in public.

- Nothing takes precedence over Sunday morning church.

- Schoolwork comes first.

- Extra money gets earned. As a single mom, I taught my boys there are no handouts.

- One day a week we do not get in the car.[11]

Note how easy it is to say no when a policy is in place. If "extra money gets earned" is a policy at your house and your kids ask for money, the answer is no—because of the policy. If you're invited to attend a conference during the summer but your policy is "to say no to any commitment that takes you away from your children in the summer," the decision is made for you—because of the policy.

Though they may be tough to uphold at first, policies make life easier in the long run. The key, of course, is to create policies that work for your family, and then make sure everyone knows what they are. It's also essential that they are evenly and consistently enforced.

Expanding and Contracting Your Vision

Expanding and contracting your vision requires making a conscious decision regarding how big your life view is going to be at any given time. For example, once I had a speaking engagement in my hometown. Since my mother lives there, I decided to take my children along so they could spend some time with Grandma.

Several weeks before the engagement, my worldview was still large. I could look at the calendar for the entire month, make plans for later in the summer, and keep an active "to do" list for the week. As the engagement approached, however, I narrowed my focus to getting my presentation ready and getting myself and the kids packed. The day before our departure, getting out the door and to Grandma's house was *all* I focused on. As soon as my presentation was over, however, I was able to expand my focus again and begin planning for our next trip—a family vacation.

You've probably used these concepts of expanding and contracting without even knowing it. Think about the last time you had friends over for dinner. When you called to extend the invitation, your life view was still large. As the day of the meal approached, your view contracted as you planned the menu and made your grocery list. The day of the event, your view likely contracted even more, to the point of being focused on straightening the house and getting the food prepared. After your guests arrived, your view could begin to expand again, and by the time they left, you were probably already thinking ahead to what the next day would bring.

Expanding and contracting your view is extremely useful in staving off stress. As I view my calendar some days, an overwhelmed feeling starts creeping over me. I simply take a deep breath (or two, or three, or ten, depending on the situation!) and ask myself, "How can I contract my focus?" Doing so keeps me from being paralyzed and gives me a focal point toward which to direct my energy.

If you're the mother of young children, expanding and contracting is an especially helpful concept for you. Your days are long, the work is hard, fatigue is ever-present, your job is sometimes thankless, and the repetition is mind-numbing. Contract your view. In the morning, focus on getting to snack time. Then focus on getting to, and through, lunch. Then, focus on getting to nap time. When you do, reward yourself with a nap of your own or 20 minutes to read or make a phone call. Then, focus on getting through supper, followed by baths and bedtime. Focusing on small segments of time will make them go faster, as opposed to looking at the expanse of an entire day spread out before you. (And remember, the season of mothering youngsters won't last forever, even though it might feel like it now!)

Utilize the "31st Day"

As you've seen by now, a balanced life doesn't just happen. It has to be worked on day in and day out. The effort requires diligence and attention and a willingness to frequently pause and ask yourself several questions. That's where the "31st Day" comes in. A glance at the calendar shows that seven months have a "31st day." A friend of mine shared that she uses the 31st of these seven months to pause and reflect. This is an idea that's worth considering for your household as well. On the thirty-first days in January, March, May, July, August, October, and December, set aside some time to ponder these questions:

- How is the overall pace of my family's life right now?
- How long has it been since we've enjoyed a family night together?
- Does our schedule allow us to eat dinner together at least four nights a week (or however many you're comfortable with)?
- When was the last time my husband and I had a chance to be alone (and awake!) together?
- Is everyone in my family (including me) getting an adequate amount of sleep?

∾ Is there something that should be taken off my family's "to do" list at this time?

The answers to these questions will provide a barometer of how you're doing in the area of balance. Is the scale tipping too far to one side? If so, make plans to rectify the situation before it spins out of control.

After you do this homework on the 31st day, here's another idea: Make it yours. Yes, you read that right. Since you spend so much time focusing on everyone else's needs, make the 31st a "Mom's Day" to do whatever you want. Read a book. Talk a walk. Treat yourself to a massage or a manicure. Go shopping. Get away with a friend. Sleep. Watch television. Go to the movies. Whatever it is you're longing to do to help you feel like a person again (instead of "just a mom"), do it. With a little advance planning, you can make all the "31st Days" yours.

If the idea of giving yourself a day off seems too radical, too generous, or too selfish, consider this: God worked for six days creating the universe, then he rested on the seventh day. Take note, girlfriend. Rest and refreshment are so important that our Creator modeled it for us. Who are we to think we can do our work as mothers without rest, when God, Master of the Universe, acknowledged the need for it?

Remember the Sabbath

Since we're talking about rest, let's talk about remembering the Sabbath. Once again the Bible provides insight into meeting our mothering needs. I already know what you're thinking, though. You'd *love* to have a day of rest each week, wouldn't you? Maybe your fairy godmother could take over for a day. Or better yet, you'd simply abandon the family for 24 hours and return rested and relaxed—and they wouldn't know you were gone. We might as well dream big, right?

Okay, I admit that talking to busy moms about the Sabbath makes me seem a little short in the IQ department. But I'm not the one who demanded that we keep the Sabbath. God did. To better understand, let's take a look at what the Bible has to say about it. The Bible clearly states that we are to observe the Sabbath. It's so important, in fact, that God made it the third of the Ten Commandments. Exodus 20:8-11 says:

> Remember the Sabbath day by keeping it holy. Six days you shall labor and do all your work, but the seventh day is a Sabbath to the LORD your God. On it you shall not do any work....For in six days the LORD made the heavens and the earth, the sea, and all that is in them, but he rested on the seventh day. Therefore, the LORD blessed the Sabbath day and made it holy.

Later in the book of Exodus, Moses told the Israelites that whoever did work on the Sabbath must be put to death (Exodus 35:2)! God is obviously serious about this commandment. So what does it mean to "do work" on the Sabbath? That's not a question I'll wrestle with here because my research into the subject shows a wide range of differing opinions. What's important is that we do indeed take time to observe the Sabbath. God worked six days, then rested on the seventh. He expects us to do the same.

What would a true day of "observing the Sabbath" look like at your house? Take the time to create a picture in your mind. If you're not currently observing the Sabbath, discuss the concept with your spouse and decide on the parameters that will govern how you choose to rest on the seventh day. Then, give yourself and your family a weekly break. You'll all benefit.

Live Your Life in Chapters

Living a balanced life is truly easier when we follow the advice in Ecclesiastes: Live it in seasons. Or, as Victoria Moran advises, "Live your life in chapters." She writes:

> When you live your life this way—focusing on one chapter now, another later—you can devote more unfettered attention to what is yours to do at this time of your life, a time that will never come again.… Chapter living is the rational way to "have it all," because when you live this way you're not expecting to have it all at once.[12]

Moran is saying that we can have it all, just not all at once. And, frankly, who would want it all at once? (A comedienne I heard asked, "If I did have it all, what would I do with it?") Having everything now would destroy your balance, and you wouldn't have anything to look forward to in the future. Yet many of us have bought into the trap of "having it all," mainly because that's what advertisers, employers, and women's groups tell us that's what we should want. But attempting to "have it all" simultaneously means our quality of life will suffer. When we embrace the concept of "chapter living," our quality of life improves and the urgency we feel about doing everything evaporates. It's a great gift. When we set priorities and make the tough decisions that keeping them requires, our efforts will ultimately be blessed.

The time you're experiencing now will *never* come again. (Of course, if your child is in the diaper stage, you might welcome this news!) Knowing that each phase of mothering will one day pass has kept many an overtired, overstressed, and overworked mother going. And knowing that tomorrow you'll be able to do what you can't do today is an important observation when it comes to heeding the advice in Ecclesiastes: There is a time for everything. The time just might not be now. Accept that fact and creating balance in your life will be easier.

How Much Is Enough?

In addition to knowing your priorities, there's an essential question that every family must ask in order to achieve the ever-elusive balance we all struggle for. The question is simple; the answer often is not. The question is: "How much is enough?"

Just because we *can* have more doesn't mean we should strive for it. Often, it is possible to have more of everything: more money, bigger houses, newer cars, more clothes, more possessions, and nicer vacations. At some point, there's a negative return on investment, and that's when we need to say, "Enough is enough."

It's not just the trap of material wealth that we fall into. It's also the activity trap. Children today have more options than ever before when it comes to deciding what they'll be involved in…and so do their parents. At what point does "just one more activity" become "too much"? That's a question that only you can answer as a family. As you wrestle with that question, strive for an overall evenness in life. Doing so means there will be times of frenzy combined with times of inactivity. The ultimate goal is to *stay the driver, not the driven*—an essential lesson we must teach our children. Doing so requires overcoming the notion that the busier we are, the more we matter. When we believe that busyness equates value, we value ourselves for what we *do* rather than for who we *are*.

We are God's children, dearly loved by our Creator. When we remember this, everything that seems so important in our lives fades away, and we can rest gently and quietly in our Father's arms. It's in his loving embrace that we can best view our lives and all our commitments in order to decide which should stay and which should go. When we do this, we'll find balance in our lives.

Collecting Our Thoughts

ᴄᴏ Balance means "the power or means to decide."

ᴄᴏ It's important to realize there is a time for everything, and a season for every activity under heaven.

ᴄᴏ The goal of balance should be to create an evenness in our lives.

ᴄᴏ Taking time to identify priorities makes balance easier to achieve.

ᴄᴏ Don't try to do more than you're capable of. Doing so causes stress.

ᴄᴏ Winnowing keeps insanity at bay.

ᴄᴏ Practice the art of saying no in order to keep things balanced.

ᴄᴏ Establishing policies helps simplify family life.

ᴄᴏ God worked six days and rested on the seventh—a schedule we should emulate.

For Group Discussion

1. How does the concept of achieving balance make you feel?

2. Describe what a balanced life looks like to you.

3. What policies do you currently have that are helpful to your family?

4. What areas of your family life could benefit from developing policies (i.e., devotion time, mealtime, getting ready-for-school time)?

5. Are you currently living your life in chapters—or are you wishing your life away? Discuss the difference.

For Personal Reflection

1. What happens to your personality, your emotions, and your physical well-being when you begin to feel out of balance?

2. Are your priorities clear in your mind? If not, take some time this week to establish a vision for yourself and your family.

3. Have you mastered the art of saying no? If not, name two techniques you can start practicing today.

4. Does giving yourself the gift of the "31st Day" appeal to you? If so, mark the next one off on your calendar now so that it is reserved for you. Enjoy it when it comes!

What Real Live Moms Say About...
Balance

"In determining what activities should be priorities for my family, I ask, 'Is it blessing this home or family? Do the children really enjoy that particular activity? Are they learning from this experience?'"

—KRISTINA NELSON

"I tend to lean too far toward 'family only' time, and that seems to suffocate my husband. So I have had to learn that it's okay to have differing interests. We don't all have to be doing everything together."

—LINDSAY DOWNS

"When I have too much to do, I reevaluate the list, and ask, 'Do I have to do these, or can someone else? Or do they have to be done at all?'"

—LOREE MUMAW

"I don't think that any family life is truly balanced. I think it's more like a seesaw, some days it's about the kids, some days it's about the husband. It's more important, I think, to be able to ride a seesaw than it is to be able to walk a balance beam."

—DORI KNIGHT

"We have to consider the viability for the whole family. For example, our youngest child was solicited for a high-ranking, travel sports team....There were fees, uniforms, and a myriad of other obligations. We determined that although our son was undoubtedly talented, the cost to the family in time and money was disproportionate to the benefit to him at this age."

—CHERYL PACILIO

4

Meeting
Your Need for
Physical Well-Being

fter I began working on this book, I met with several mothers' groups to determine if I was on track with the topics I planned to address. All of the groups, without exception, said they *didn't* want to read a chapter about exercise. It was clear from the comments I heard that just the thought of breaking a sweat caused anxiety, despair, and depression—all at once! That's why this is a chapter on physical well-being, not just exercise, though the latter is important to achieving overall well-being.

There is a fair amount of activity that comes with being a homemaker—doing laundry, emptying the dishwasher, making the beds, scrubbing the floor, vacuuming, and washing windows. And the list goes on. But I'm not talking about this kind of physical activity here. I *am* talking about the physical activity that elevates your heart rate, clears your mind, *and* soothes your soul. And don't forget the importance of rest in contributing to physical well-being!

Before you read on, let me tell you what I'm *not* going to cover in this chapter. I'm not going to write about "Ten Ways to Lose Your Baby Weight Faster" or "Look Like a Super-Model in Five

Easy Steps." You can get that type of information at the newsstand or at the checkout counter at the grocery store. I'm also not going to make you feel guilty for what you're *not* doing. (The fact is, if you're the mother of young children, you're likely in "survival" mode, and your physical well-being is the last thing on your mind.) I will provide some ideas for meeting your need for physical activity—outside of hauling an infant carrier, moving a newborn from one breast to the other, hefting toddlers throughout the day, pushing a child on a swing at the park, or hauling children from the backseat of the car up to bed (without waking them of course!).

Taking time to pursue your own physical well-being may seem selfish to you. It used to seem that way to me, too. But after talking to a lot of stressed-out, burned-out, exhausted, and overwhelmed moms, I now see it as an investment in family. Every minute I spend exercising or resting returns itself many times over in the form of increased patience, a positive attitude, and the energy necessary to keep up with managing a household and meeting my family's needs. I like to think of the investment in my well-being as a plan for "surthrival." Together, physical activity and rest make it possible for me to survive *and* thrive as a mother.

Let's take a minute to see what the Bible says about the bodies that house our souls. The most well-known verses regarding caring for your body may be 1 Corinthians 6:19-20: "Do you not know that your body is a temple of the Holy Spirit, who is in you, whom you have received from God? You are not your own; you were bought at a price. Therefore honor God with your body." Romans 12:1 says, "Therefore, I urge you, brothers, in view of God's mercy, to offer your bodies as living sacrifices, holy and pleasing to God—this is your spiritual act of worship."

Does it change your outlook when you realize that your body is a temple of the Holy Spirit and that we should offer our bodies as living sacrifices to God? When viewed in light of these verses, caring for your physical well-being becomes an act of spiritual worship, not selfishness (as long as you don't take it to an extreme). This should make it easier for you to make it a priority to get the rest and exercise you need.

A Word to the Sedentary

If you are not currently exercising, or not doing so on a regular basis, I hope you'll consider making it a priority. I'm not talking about training for a marathon, but simply ensuring that your body is up and moving as much as possible each day. If you are challenged by illness and/or physical limitations, focus on what you can do, rather than what you can't. Take a lesson from a friend of mine, Wendy Housel, who was diagnosed with rheumatoid arthritis at the age of 23. She's had repeated surgeries, but she keeps on going. Though her legs are in braces, she doesn't let that stop her. I see her out almost daily walking her greyhound, Faith. Though there is much she can't do, Wendy chooses to focus on what she can do. She's an inspiration to those around her, especially me.

If you do choose to add exercise to your life, start slowly. "Slow but sure" is the healthiest way to add or increase the amount of physical exercise you're doing. When you start slowly, you're more likely to stick with it, rather than pushing yourself to extremes and then giving up on your fitness goals because you're overly sore or exhausted. Remember, too, that small efforts make a big difference in the well-being arena. If you're planning to increase your level of physical activity, take it one day at a time and add a little at a time. That's the safest way to live an active life.

If you have not been exercising on a regular basis, experts recommend consulting your doctor before you begin to do so. This is especially important if you're currently under a doctor's care, have a family history of illness, or have personal health concerns. If you're not exercising and wish to begin, or are exercising but want to increase the length or intensity of your workouts, the following ideas regarding how to fit fitness into your schedule may be helpful.

Sunday-Night Scheduling

When I ask women what the biggest barrier to ensuring their physical well-being is, the answer is almost always the same: *Time.* I hear it again and again. "I don't have time." "I'm too busy!" There's a myth about taking care of our physical bodies. It says that it is going to be difficult, and it will take a lot of time. That's not true! While many fitness experts recommend at least 30 minutes of exercise per day, research has shown that three 10-minute chunks of physical activity are just as effective as one 30-minute workout.

Can you find a few minutes in your day? That's all I'm asking you to do. Here's why: When it comes to physical activity, *something* is better than *nothing*. If you can't exercise for an hour, squeeze in 40 minutes of activity. If you can't do 40 minutes, do 30. (By the way, 30 minutes constitutes only two percent of your day. Certainly you can spare that, can't you?) If you can't do 30, do 20. And if you can't find 20 minutes in your day, find 10 minutes. If you can't even find 10 minutes in your day for fitness, author and speaker Susie Larson recommends doing push-ups against the counter in your kitchen while you're waiting for the microwave to finish its work![1] Why? Because *something is better than nothing.*

If you've ever caught yourself saying the words "I don't have time" when it comes to exercise, stop right there. The truth is, we're all so busy that nobody "has" time. You have to "make" time—like you do for any other priority in your life. *Time to tend to your well-being has to be scheduled*, just like any other appointment.

I challenge you to do something nice for your body. Pull out your calendar right now and schedule 10 minutes for exercise sometime *today*—maybe while your children are napping or after dinner when your husband or a neighbor can watch the children. Better yet, put this book down right now and do some sit-ups or push-ups! As the old Nike shoe commercial said, "Just do it." And keep doing it. At the beginning of each week, schedule your exercise for the week, even if it's just 10 minutes worth of physical activity a day.

If you're like other women I know, here's what will happen. Eventually, your 10 minutes will turn into 12, then 15, then 30 minutes, and perhaps even an hour for exercise. You'll have more energy and think more clearly. As a result, your tolerance level with your kids will increase. If you do this long enough, your stamina will also increase, and you'll recognize other health benefits as well, including weight control, toned muscles, and strong bones. In addition, physical activity lowers the risk of developing heart disease, osteoporosis, arthritis, diabetes, and breast, colon, and uterine cancer.

Though the immediate benefit for your family may be lower stress and more energy for you, the long-term benefits are even more important: a healthier mom who is likely to be around for high school and college graduations, weddings, and the joy of holding grandchildren. That's great incentive to get off the couch and start moving, don't you think?

What Can *You Do?*

If you've tried to fit exercise into your schedule previously but haven't been able to do so successfully, you may require a shift in your thinking. First, physical activity must become a priority—

right up there with caring for your family. Second, you must embrace the power of possibility thinking, which requires changing "I can't" into "I *can*." Let's pretend it's Sunday night, and you're ready to schedule your workouts for the week. (Remember, these can be 10-minute workouts or 90-minute workouts. The important thing is that you're moving your body!) As you look at the calendar and all you have to do this week, you may think, *There's no way I can fit this into my schedule. I just can't do it!* Whenever you hear the word "can't," counter with this: "Maybe not. But I *can* _____." You fill in the blank. Maybe you can find 10 minutes to walk around the block. Better yet, maybe you can find 30 minutes. Whatever it is, do it. Remember, with exercise a *little goes a long way* and *something is better than nothing.*

Find a Workout Buddy

When Pat Essig's twin daughters began preschool, Pat took the opportunity to start exercising regularly. Knowing she would be more likely to keep her commitment if she had a friend to work out with, Pat invited a neighbor to start walking with her. Being committed to her friend helps get Pat out the door, even on days when she doesn't feel like it. Pat's discovered the power of having a workout buddy, someone to exercise with who will help motivate her to look after her own well-being. Is there someone like this in your life? When looking for an exercise partner, look for:

- someone you're comfortable being around
- someone who is reliable
- someone who exercises at a similar pace or workout level
- someone who is an encourager
- someone who will not compete with you

Having a workout partner isn't for everyone. If you prefer to be alone, or your exercise schedule is irregular, having a partner may cause more stress than it is worth. If, however, your intentions to exercise are good, but your ability to follow through is lacking, you might benefit from committing to exercise with a friend.

Trading Spaces

During this season in your life, your best workout partner might not actually work out *with* you. Instead, he or she may simply make it possible for you to work out—and vice versa. My husband is my best workout partner, but we don't exercise at the same time. Instead, we've agreed to help each other meet our fitness goals simply by taking turns being with our children so that the other can work out freely. We alternate workout times and days. On the weekends, one of us may exercise early on Saturday, so the other can exercise in the afternoon. Or, one will head to the gym on Saturday, and the other will exercise on Sunday after church. During the week, I go during the day when possible, then commit to being home at least one evening so that my husband can go to the gym after work.

Though it's nice to have a spouse as a workout partner, don't be discouraged if it's not a possibility in your family. Perhaps another family member (your mom, a sibling, or an aunt, uncle, or grandparent?) would be willing to give you the gift of some time to exercise. Or maybe you can exchange babysitting with a similarly minded friend who'd be willing to watch your children in return for a free morning at the gym for herself.

Be a Joiner

If you lack motivation to be active, join a club. A financial commitment may be enough to get you out the door. When you join a health club, determine what the average cost of a trip to the gym is. If you know you're paying $4.85 per visit, it will be harder to skip your workouts (as opposed to foregoing a free walk around the neighborhood). Other ideas of something to join include dance classes, karate, and boxing.

If a financial commitment doesn't motivate you, maybe a team sport will. I played on a recreational volleyball league and dragged myself to the gym several nights when I would have rather stayed home—simply because I felt obligated to my teammates. Usually after just a few volleys I'd perk up and be glad I showed up.

Making a commitment to others—or to your pocketbook— may supply the motivation you need to follow through on your intentions to be active.

Develop a Backup Workout

As a mother, there are going to be times when even the most carefully planned days will go awry. Kids have a special radar, I'm certain, and it seems they get sick on the days when you have the most to do, doesn't it?

Joe Sweeney, a personal fitness trainer and author of *I Know I Should Exercise, But...7 Steps to Removing Your "But" from Exercise,* suggests developing a "Ten-Minute Anywhere Workout." Joe's workout consists of push-ups, abdominal exercises, and back strengtheners. He does two sets of 15 to 20 repetitions of each strength exercise, followed by ten stretching exercises. He does the workout every other day, no matter where he is.[2]

We can adapt Joe's philosophy by assuming there are days when we won't be able to work out—even if we want to. Be prepared for these days in advance, and then your workouts won't get interrupted. Consider creating your own "Ten-Minute Anywhere Workout" or investing in a few workout videos for rainy days or when a child's illness keeps you house bound. Or find out if your cable TV company offers free fitness videos such as ten-minute abdominal, buns, or total body workouts. Then you can work out in the comfort of your own home at no additional charge. Having a backup plan conveniently available makes it easier to keep your body moving, even when you can't get out of the house.

"Commercial Stretching"

Another great idea from Joe is "Commercial Stretching."[3] Instead of sitting through television commercials, Joe suggests stretching through them. During the first commercial break, walk around your house to warm up. Then, stretch through the remainder of the commercial breaks. (Better yet, why not stretch while you watch the rest of the program?) Joe recommends easing slowly into each stretch, breathing deeply, and holding the stretch for about 20 seconds or until it becomes uncomfortable. Avoid bouncing in order to prevent injury. Involve your children in "Commercial Stretching" as well. Not only will you be setting a good example, you may also help them develop healthier lifelong TV viewing habits.

Include Your Children

Picture this: One summer I was so desperate for the opportunity to move my body (in ways other than serving my children) that I loaded my kids' bikes and helmets into the car and drove to the running track at a school near our home. I took the bikes out of the car, put helmets on the kids, and lined us up for a race. "On your mark. Get set. Go!" I shouted. And off we went: my children on their bikes while I jogged behind. Around and around the track we went, my kids squealing every time they passed me, which was frequently.

How can you include your children so you can exercise? As moms, we have to be creative in this regard. A friend of mine diligently exercised during her kids' soccer practices. While they dribbled and practiced kicking goals, she race-walked around the perimeter of the park. When practice was over, she was able to mark two things off her agenda! Another friend's husband is an avid biker. Not to be left behind, she and her twin daughters have purchased bikes and the family now rides together. In fact, she and her daughters are training for a future family biking vacation.

Many gyms and sport complexes are responding to the parental exercise dilemma by offering child care. And now, while parents exercise, kids can exercise, too, since some gyms offer "kid fit" programs involving rock climbing, games, and other activities designed to be both fun and healthy for youngsters.

Young children can accompany you during your workouts as observers in a stroller or wagon as you're walking or jogging. Older children can join you playing tennis, hiking, swimming, or skiing.

It takes work to make time to exercise when children are in the picture, but it can be done. Don't let them become an excuse for ignoring your own physical well-being. Remember, it's *because* of them that we want to be healthy. Your children should be an incentive to exercise, not an obstacle.

Water Intake and Nutrition

Though physical activity is important to your well-being, your body's health is also heavily influenced by what you eat and drink. Sadly, many moms are more concerned about what their kids are eating and drinking and often forget to look out for their own needs. I'm not a dietician, so it would be unwise for me to try to impart nutritional advice. However, I'll remind you of a couple of things. First, eating leftovers off your children's plates does not necessarily constitute a balanced diet for you. Also, skipping meals or forgetting to eat can mess with your metabolism. If you're guilty of either of these offenses, commit to changing your eating habits.

Another aspect of health has to do with water intake. I know that I don't drink enough. How about you? It's recommended that we drink at least 64 ounces per day, an amount I find hard to drink. It's something I'm aspiring to, however. I also learned recently that we should drink water *before* we are thirsty. If we wait until we are parched, our body's fluids are already depleted. Consequently, we should be drinking water regularly throughout the day.

Balancing Physical Activity with Rest

Despite the importance of exercise, physical well-being isn't just about how much we move our bodies, or how many calories we burn, or whether or not we've reached our ideal weight. It *is* about honoring our body's needs, whether it is for food, exercise, or rest. This last issue is just as important—or maybe even more important—as the issue of exercise. Without rest, our bodies aren't strong enough to produce the energy we need to exercise. They also aren't strong enough to be up to the mental and physical tasks of mothering.

"Whoa," you say. "I haven't had a good night's sleep since I became a mother. What's this about needing enough sleep to be a good mother?" According to the National Sleep Foundation, 47 million Americans are not getting enough sleep each night. In 2002, the Foundation did a survey, asking respondents how they are affected by not sleeping enough. Here's what they found: Not surprisingly, those who got fewer than six hours of sleep were more likely to say they were tired than those getting more than eight hours of sleep. People also reported they were:

ꕥ *twice* more likely to describe themselves as stressed

ꕥ *twice* more likely to describe themselves as sad

ꕥ nearly *three* times more likely to describe themselves as angry[4]

Take a look at those words: *stressed, sad,* and *angry.* Now put them in the context of motherhood. Do you want to be a stressed, sad, and angry mother? Is that the example you want your children to emulate? Is that the legacy you wish to provide for them? I didn't think so.

If you're not getting enough sleep every night (and what mother of young children is?), you are more likely to spend each day stressed, sad, and angry. That's a dangerous combination. Wouldn't you rather start each day well-rested, content, and joyful? I would. That's why we place such a huge emphasis on a good night's sleep at our house.

Sleep Requirements

You might be surprised to know how much sleep you need at various stages of life. According to the National Sleep Foundation, babies need 15 hours of sleep each night. Grade-schoolers need 9-13 hours. (Is your grade-schooler getting this? Most don't.) Teenagers need 8-10 hours. (Most teenagers aren't getting enough sleep, either. No wonder they are often sullen, grumpy, and disrespectful!) Adults need between 7-9 hours a night.[5] (How much sleep did *you* get last night?)

If you need eight hours of sleep a night, don't trick yourself into believing it is okay to get seven because the adult range is seven to nine hours of sleep. Your sleep needs don't disappear just because you think you should be able to get by on less. In fact, the less you get, the more you'll need to "get caught up." (If you're not

sure how much you need, you can measure your sleep requirements midway through your next vacation. Don't set an alarm,
wake up on your own, and see how much sleep you naturally need
without the press of school and/or job. It's important to do this
midway through your vacation so you have time to unwind after
the stress of preparing, packing, and traveling.)

I envy people who only need six or less hours of sleep a night,
but I am not one of them. Consequently, it would be foolish and
self-deceptive for me to sleep less than I need to. More importantly, it's not fair to other family members if my lack of sleep
affects my ability to be mentally alert, loving, and helpful. If you're
not getting enough sleep and your sleep deficit is manifesting itself
in grumpiness, unkindness, short-temperedness, stress, sadness,
and anger, it's time to come clean with yourself and start getting
the rest you need—tonight.

Remember earlier in this chapter we discussed focusing on
what you *can* do? Let's think about that in relation to getting
enough sleep. If you can't get the eight hours you need tonight,
could you start by going to bed five minutes earlier than last night?
Do this for a week. Then next week, go to bed five minutes earlier
again (which is now ten minutes earlier than your current bedtime). Keep moving the time up until you're getting enough sleep.
Healthy individuals who are sleeping enough regularly wake
before their alarm clock sounds.

Master the Art of the 20-Minute Nap

Sleep isn't just for nighttime. In college, I discovered how beneficial a catnap during the day can be. After hearing a radio report
about the value of a brief nap, I mastered what I call "The Art of
the 20-Minute Nap." Desperate to keep up with my studies and
other commitments, I regularly snuck up to the third floor of my
sorority house, which housed rows and rows of bunk beds where

we slept in a common dorm. I'd climb into my designated bed, set my alarm for 20 minutes and doze off. Because of that early training, now I can lie down, sleep anywhere from 18 to 22 minutes, and wake up without an alarm, feeling refreshed. Though college was eons ago, I'm still napping. I count on a 20-minute nap to get me through the day when my energy lags.

Here's what you need to know in order to benefit from a 20-minute nap. Not everyone is able to wake up on her own, so I suggest setting an alarm. Although your first forays into brief naps may not immediately help you feel refreshed, please don't give up on the idea of napping. It takes 21 days to create a new habit, so you may have to "practice" napping for a while. You may find it helpful to invest in a sleep mask to make it easier to fall asleep. I use one when I nap—partly to cut out the light, but mostly as a signal to my body that it's time to sleep. Masks are inexpensive and can be found at many drugstores and stores that specialize in body pampering.

Setting the Stage for Sleep

If you have young children who still nap, finding time for your own nap will be easy. But what if your children are no longer napping? Does that mean no naps for you? No way! Even if your children aren't napping, they can still benefit from taking a mandatory break each day. After naps stopped at our house, we still had quiet time. During quiet time, each of us (me included) had to spend 20 to 30 minutes in our respective bedrooms. The rules were simple: You could read or play quietly, but you had to be on your bed. Confining kids to the bed prevented rowdy or wild play, and it also had another effect. Often, my children would fall asleep even when they claimed they weren't tired. Though quiet time is no longer mandatory on a daily basis, we still use it occasionally to slow the family's pace when necessary or when fatigue is evident.

If you work outside the home in an environment that's not conducive to taking a nap, refresh your mood by taking a brisk walk on your lunch hour or taking the stairs instead of the elevator. Park farther away than necessary when attending meetings so that you can take a few extra steps before heading inside. If you have a private office, hang a "Do Not Disturb" sign on your door when necessary during breaks or your lunch hour and close your eyes for a few moments of rest. Be sure to set an alarm, however, so you're not caught napping on the job!

Benefits of Sleep for Children

Sleep problems are often interrelated in a family. In other words, if children aren't sleeping, then parents aren't likely to be either. If parents don't set a good sleep example, then children are less likely to develop good sleep habits. That's why it is crucial that a family commitment be made to getting enough sleep. I'm an advocate for teaching children to go to sleep on their own and in their own bed because helping children develop healthy sleep habits now is more likely to lead to healthy sleep habits when they are older.

Dozens of books have been written about the topic of getting children to sleep, so I won't address the hows and whys here. I do want to call your attention to the sleep requirements again. Take a look at the following chart:

Babies	15 hours
Grade schoolers	9-13 hours
Teenagers	8-10 hours
Adults	7-9 hours

Are your children getting enough sleep?

These days I'm concerned about the number of kids' activities that go late into the evening, making it practically impossible to get a child to bed at a reasonable hour. It's possible that you may have to exert your influence in this area, picking your children up early from late activities and explaining why you're doing so. We've opted out of several activities that required our children to be up later than they should be at the various ages of their development.

Unless there is an underlying medical condition, many behavior problems in children stem from hunger or fatigue. The good news is that you can do something about both of these. Make sure your kids eat regularly (nourishing food, of course!), and make sure they get enough sleep. You'll save yourself lots of parenting trouble if you do.

If you know that your children aren't getting enough sleep, do the same with them that you're doing for yourself. Set bedtime five minutes earlier and continue doing so until your children can wake refreshed in the morning. It's not only a gift to them, it's a gift to you…and all the other people they come into contact with during the day.

Recommit to Physical Well-Being

Motherhood, by its very nature, requires us to be active. Sure, breast-feeding burns calories, but it's a sedentary activity. Changing diapers and doing laundry requires moving our muscles, but it doesn't get us out into the sunshine and fresh air. Helping with homework requires us to use our minds, but it doesn't necessarily help clear them. And at a time when sleep and rest are crucial, we may find both in short supply.

Adequate rest and exercise won't just happen. We have to *make* them. Start today by setting aside ten minutes for exercise (if not more) and five minutes for going to bed earlier tonight. Be kind to your body, and it will be more kind to you.

Remember, our bodies are a temple of the Holy Spirit. As such, they should be well cared for. Romans 12:1 tells us our bodies are also "living sacrifices." What kind of sacrifice are you presenting? One that's fatigued and in need of physical activity? Or one that's healthy and well rested? Though it may be hard to present the latter to God, it is possible. Ultimately, the choice is up to you.

Collecting Our Thoughts

- Time to care for your physical health should be scheduled, just like any other appointment.

- Focusing on what you *can* do will enable you to do the things you think you can't.

- Kids should not be an excuse for why we can't exercise. Instead, they should be the reason we do exercise.

- Rest is an important and essential part of self-care.

- A 20-minute nap can be refreshing—and gives you the energy you need when you don't think you can make it through the day.

For Group Discussion

1. How does your outlook about your physical well-being change when you think about your body as a temple of the Holy Spirit?

2. How can we offer our bodies "as living sacrifices to God"?

3. What strategies have you used successfully to help you make time to exercise?

4. Do you take naps? Discuss your feelings (negative or positive) about naps.

5. How does focusing on what you *can* do change your life?

For Personal Reflection

1. How can you apply the idea that "something is better than nothing" when it comes to caring for your physical well-being?

2. Would you benefit from having a workout partner? If so, who are some possibilities?

3. What kinds of exercises can you conveniently do at home? Make a list and have it handy for the days your schedule gets interrupted.

4. Are you and your children getting enough sleep? If not, develop a plan to change that—starting tonight!

What Real Live Moms Say About...
Physical Well-Being

"I love our local YMCA. They have wonderful, free child care for members while you work out. I drop off my oldest at preschool, the youngest goes into the nursery, and I work out. And it's all for about $30 a month! It is awesome 'me' time even if I do have to share it with a bunch of sweaty people!"

—AMY KENNEDY

"My husband and I enjoy biking on the weekends, and fortunately, our daughter enjoys her bike trailer. I also have been known to do an aerobic tape...during our daughter's nap when pressed for time."

—ASHLEY R.

"On Sunday evenings, the church we're attending has a program for school-age children—and it's awesome—but we don't usually go because getting the kids to bed at a decent time is important to me. Otherwise, it's hard to get them up in the morning."

—HEATHER ADAMS

～

"I'm a snacker and find it hard to eat the healthiest snacks, particularly with cravings (which I have whether I am pregnant or not). I try not to buy anything that is not healthy. I am working on adjusting my entire family to a better way of eating."

—KIM L.

～

"I exercise at the YMCA while my son takes swimming lessons twice a week. I also bike and take walks with my son."

—DEB S.

～

"I tend to eat worse if I haven't exercised, which makes me not want to exercise, which makes me eat even worse. I know that I do this— I just haven't been able to break the cycle. Plus, I *hate* to sweat!"

—TAMARA AHRENS

5

Meeting
Your Need for
Order

I had no idea that kids came with so much stuff! Whether you have one child or six, the system you used to minimize chaos in your life before children won't necessarily work after kids come along. That painful truth hit me one day after I spent over an hour searching for my car keys. After I gave up looking for the keys, I picked up the carrier to take it (and my sleeping baby) upstairs—and there were my lost keys.

And I'm not alone. Do you know that the average human spends one year of his or her life looking for lost and/or misplaced items? (I swear I've spent that much time alone looking for lost soccer shoes or the match to a sock I'm holding!) But when we're late for a soccer game, or the bus is headed down the street to pick up our children, who has a year to look for something?

Life with children is chaotic. There's no other way to describe it. Even the best laid plans go awry when Junior has misplaced his homework or can't find his shin guards. Or when you're in the midst of caring for an ailing parent, shuttling between home, school, and the hospital, and suddenly remember it's your turn to provide snacks for Girl Scouts. Or when you have three children who have sporting events simultaneously, all at different sports complexes. The sooner you accept the chaos that accompanies a life with children, the easier it will be to thrive in the midst of it.

Admitting to the chaos recognizes its presence in my life, acknowledges its nature, and assumes it is going to be present as long as there are children in my home. My job, as I see it, is to order it as best as I can so that I minimize its effects on family life. That's where minimizing chaos, or, as I like to think of it, creating "organized" chaos comes in. The idea of "organized" chaos allows me to believe that I can, in fact, have some control over what goes on in my life and the lives of my children.

There is tension that comes with creating order. Too much of it leads to overly rigid schedules and plans; too little leads to hurriedness, disorganization, and unnecessary stress. The key, as in most things in life, is finding a balance that takes into account your "chaos personality" as well as what's comfortable and realistic for you as chief organizer for your family.

We can create order and reduce the mother load by taking eight steps. These steps conveniently spell out UNLOAD IT, my mantra for simplifying things. You see, it's the accumulation of things (things we own or things we do) that create chaos and disorder in our lives. When something begins to spin out of control, we can *unload it* by following these steps and restoring order to our family life. Doing so not only makes today more pleasant and tomorrow more manageable, it also teaches children valuable life skills. And, remember, the end purpose of bearing the mother load is to raise responsible, independent children.

Unload It

Here's a brief overview of the UNLOAD IT steps for creating and maintaining order:

1. Understand and accept your chaos personality

2. Nip it in the bud

3. Lead the way

4. Organize what you can

5. Anchor it

6. Do it now!

7. Involve your family

8. Take stock

When you follow these steps, you'll live a more orderly and controlled life. There is a key to successfully doing so: You must understand and accept that you're never done with the process of unloading. You can't do it once and expect the fruits of your labor to carry you through the remaining days of your life. Unloading works best when it becomes a habit—a way of life that illuminates your path, frees your mind, and reduces your burden. UNLOAD IT is about taking control, creating systems, simplifying, and eliminating that which doesn't work, and passing these skills on to your children. Most of all, it requires acknowledging that you do have control—even when you feel out of it.

Are you ready to UNLOAD IT? If so, let's go!

Step 1: Understand and Accept Your Chaos Personality

Before you read any further, I want you to put this book down, go look in the mirror, smile at yourself and say, "I love you—just the way you are." I'll wait while you do this.

Did you do it? Good.

"I love you—just the way you are." You've probably said these words, or something similar, to your children when they begin to recognize their shortcomings or wish God had created them a little differently. Your acceptance of each child—just as he or she is—recognizes each child as a miracle and acknowledges God's wisdom in packaging your child the way he did. In order to be fair to ourselves, we must be willing to accept ourselves the way we are, too. That's why the first step in the process of unloading is to "understand and accept your chaos personality."

Notice that Step 1 isn't to change your personality or to identify your shortcomings. Instead, we're going to work with who you are, rather than trying to change you.

Each of us has the ability to manage our family and create organized chaos—in our own way. You might be able to do so with flair and panache. Or it might not come easily to you. But each of us has the ability. We simply need to be honest about how we are naturally and what's comfortable for us as we tackle the chore of creating order in our life together as a family.

As we get ready to study the various types of chaos personalities, remember this: None is better than the others, and none is the "right" way to be. We are all different, and identifying our personality type is simply a means to help us create a system that will work most effectively for us. Take a look at the following three chaos personality types, and see which one you identify with most.

At one end of the spectrum, we have the *Organized Neatnik*. This individual thrives on organizing and is good at it. Being organized comes naturally to her, and she enjoys it. She's a meticulous planner. She is able to find things she needs easily, is orderly in how she organizes things, and doesn't mind spending time creating and using the systems necessary to creating structure.

While being an Organized Neatnik has its benefits, it also has its dark side. Neatniks can be obsessive, inflexible, and easily flustered when a system or plan fails. They may try to force others to adhere to their system of organization (even if it is counter-intuitive to the others). Some Neatniks also exhibit a tremendous amount of control in the area of organization because it makes up for lack of control in other areas of their lives. This is not necessarily bad, but understanding why a Neatnik needs to be in control is helpful to understanding her. Finally, some Neatniks miss spending time developing their relationships because they are so busy managing things.

In the middle of the spectrum is the *Organized Messy.* This individual flirts with organization—when it is convenient. She often will let things slide, then do something about "getting organized" when she can no longer stand the chaos or can't locate something she needs. This personality type is also a planner, but is not as rigid or meticulous as the Organized Neatnik. Organizing does not come as easily to her. This personality type often files in "piles"—where she knows she can find something, but not with the same ease as a Neatnik.

The downside of being an Organized Messy is that this style of organization is often "schizophrenic." One day things are arranged by color, one day alphabetically, and one day simply by commingling everything in a plastic tub. Organization is not consistent, sometimes leading to a false sense of security—until it's time to leave for the soccer game and no soccer shoes can be found. The other weakness of this personality type is that an Organized Messy is methodical enough to appear to have her act together, but not organized enough to eliminate all unnecessary chaos.

On the other end of the chaos personality spectrum is the *Laid-Back Lackadaisical.* This personality type regularly flies by the seat of her pants and believes that organization takes too much time and too much work. More interested in building relation-ships than in managing things, the Laid-Back Lackadaisical rarely plans more than five minutes in advance and, as a result, often operates in a crisis mode. Flexible and easygoing, the Laid-Back Lackadaisical is easy to get along with. Lackadaisicals make great friends because they aren't distracted by the need to manage and organize.

Due to her relaxed nature, however, the Laid-Back Lack-adaisical experiences more chaos than either of the other two per-sonality types. Laid-Back Lackadaisicals often can't find the things they need. They live with needless clutter, tell themselves they'll "get organized" tomorrow, and often neglect deadlines—resulting in late fees, missed opportunities (such as kids' summer camps that fill up before the Lackadaisical can get her registration in), or inconveniences (such as having telephone service disconnected due to failure to pay the bill or running out of gas on the highway). All of this leads to stress—most of which is unnecessary.

Which personality type are you? Be honest in your assessment. It doesn't do any good to identify yourself as being something you're not. Each of the personality types has some good charac-teristics, and each has some "growth edges" (a nice way to say "weaknesses"). For example, if you're a Neatnik, your rigid nature and attention to detail may cause stress for your family, and you may need to work at being more flexible. Or, if you're an Orga-nized Messy, you may need to be more consistent in adhering to the organizational systems you've created for your family. Finally, if you're a Laid-Back Lackadaisical, you might need to play less with your children so that you have the time necessary to make sure there is order in your family.

Note that there are also extremes in each personality type. For example, there are Really Organized Neatniks, Organized Neatniks, and Not-As-Organized Neatniks. All are more organized than Organized Messies, but to varying degrees.

As you can guess, Really Organized Neatniks are the most rigid and least flexible. Not-So-Organized Neatniks are still Neatniks but they are closer to Organized Messies than they are to Really Organized Neatniks. Once you've identified your chaos personality, you'll gain further insight into yourself if you can also determine which extreme, if either, you are closest to.

Remember, none of the personality types is right, and none is best. They simply are. Understanding and acknowledging your personality type is important so that you can identify your strengths and weaknesses for the purpose of approaching the ideas that follow in this chapter in a way that is comfortable and realistic for you. Organized Neatniks may already be implementing many (or most!) of the ideas and easily embrace those they aren't currently using. Laid-Back Lackadaisicals may wince at the ideas that require planning and organization but adapt others that can be accomplished quickly and conveniently. In other words, I'm depending on you to identify the best ideas in this chapter *for you, according to your personality type.* Embrace, implement, and adapt the ideas that speak to you.

Step 2: Nip It in the Bud

The more stuff (not only does this refer to material things, it also refers to intangible commitments) you have, the more there is to manage. Remember, you do not have to manage, or organize, what does not enter your home. Consequently, a good piece of chaos management advice is to "nip it in the bud." In other words, refuse to own (or bring into your home) anything you do not want to be responsible for.

Become an advocate for minimizing your "stuff," and you'll automatically reduce the opportunity for disorganization and chaos to reign in your house. The more you work to control what you can, the less the rest (what you can't control) will stress you. Here are some practical suggestions on how to "nip it in the bud." Hopefully, you'll think of others as you read through these ideas.

Take your name off marketing lists. To reduce the amount of junk mail you get, send a postcard to the Mail Preference Service, operated by the Direct Marketing Association, requesting that your name be removed from mailing lists. (Although it takes about three months before you'll see a reduction in the amount of mail you receive, your name will stay on the list for five years.) When writing to the Mail Preference Service, include your name, address, signature, and a listing of all the different ways your name appears on mailing labels (Susan Smith, Susie Smith, Sue Smith). Send your request to the Mail Preference Service, ATTN: Department 14030563, Direct Marketing Association, P.O. Box 282, Carmel, New York 10512. There is no cost for this service. You can also register your name online, although there is a $5 charge for the convenience of doing so. Go to http://www.the-dma.org and click on "For Consumers." There, you'll also be able to remove your name from telephone lists and e-mail lists.

Another option is to sign up for the National Do Not Call Registry, sponsored by the federal government. Simply go to http://www.donotcall.gov and register your phone number. There is no cost, and registration is good for five years. The "Do Not Call" law does exempt some types of organizations, so you might still hear from local merchants, religious and charitable organizations, professional and alumni associations, political candidates and office holders. When you do hear from any of these groups, simply ask that your name be added to their internal "Do Not Call" list. Most will honor your desire not to be disturbed.

For those catalogs that still come through the mail, or those unsolicited e-mails that show up in your mailbox, be consistent in replying with "Unsubscribe" in the subject line or in calling the 800 number on the catalog and asking to be removed from the mailing list. Doing so now will minimize the stuff you have to manage later.

Sort your mail over the recycle bin daily. Recycle junk mail, catalogs you won't order from (remember to call the 800 number first to have your name removed from the list!), and other advertisements. Put bills-to-be-paid where you know you will see them, and magazines where you'll look for them when you are ready to read them. Respond to invitations as quickly as possible, then put them where you'll be able to find them as the event approaches. Sort your mail *every* day. In fact, make it a habit to do it the minute the mail comes in from the mailbox. Tossing out will minimize what stays in your home. Doing it every day will prevent accumulation—and the overwhelming feeling that comes with it.

Learn to say no. We discussed the importance of learning to say no in the chapter on balance. It's applicable here, too. Don't say yes to anything you don't want to have to manage or spend time on. Saying yes to owning a pet means feeding and cleaning. A rock collection requires space to store or display it. Being a Girl Scout leader means planning and organizing meetings. If whatever you're considering enhances your life or that of a family members, helps you meet a goal, or is something you're good at and/or like to do, say yes. If it doesn't fit into one of these categories, carefully consider nipping it in the bud.

Change the way you celebrate. I love a good birthday party as much as the next mom, but I despise all the toys that enter our house as a result. More toys mean more clutter and more things to manage. Our closets and playroom are already overflowing. As each birthday brings more stuff, I seem to get further and further behind in my ability to manage it. We've solved the solution (sort of) by alternating "friends" birthday parties with "family only" parties. This way, we minimize the number of presents that enter our house. I wish I had the courage to start a "no gifts please" birthday tradition at my kids' birthday parties, like many adults do. Then we could celebrate freely with friends without worrying about where we'll put the stuff they bring in the form of gifts. My kids did go to a unique party recently where each child brought a present for a gift exchange rather than bringing a gift for the birthday child. This way, each child received a gift (including the birthday boy), and it made a treat bag unnecessary (another source of stuff!).

Another way to eliminate the flood of gifts that usually show up at a kid's party is to either limit the number of guests (which is often hard to do) or to ask for a donation to a charity in lieu of a gift. A friend of mine told me about a party her nephew went to. The birthday boy asked each guest to bring a blanket for distribution at a homeless shelter. Then, during the party, the boy's father took the guests to the shelter so each child could participate in the blanket distribution. Believe it or not, the idea for this party came from the boy!

Finally, consider asking for "educational and experience" gifts instead of toys. I've asked family members to consider giving gifts that allow our children to learn or experience something. We especially appreciate books that help develop reading skills; craft kits that encourage hands-on activity; and gift certificates that allow us to experience things together, such as going out for ice cream or bowling. This doesn't mean my children never get toys. (They get plenty!) But it does help reduce the number of new things we bring into our home each year.

Now it's your turn. What's come into your home lately that you'd rather not have to manage? What's there that you don't want any more of? Make a mental note and practice the art of nipping it in the bud. Doing so will make your future as a family more manageable.

Step 3: Lead the Way

Your children are learning from you each and every day. They are absorbing how you respond to chaos and how you work to create order in your home. If they like what they see, they'll likely adopt your habits. If they don't like what they see, they'll make a decision (consciously or otherwise) to do things differently. You can help them develop healthy patterns by leading the way for them. This means establishing routines for them and then honoring these routines by sticking to them. For instance, a bedtime routine lets children know what you expect and when you expect it. At our house, the bedtime routine consists of a bath or shower (unless one is unnecessary), a snack, teeth brushing, a bedtime story, then prayers and kisses and hugs goodnight. Because we rarely deviate from this routine, bedtime is easy at our house. (We even ask our babysitters to follow this same routine.) Bedtime is orderly because we lead the way for our children with a routine. When are routines good to establish? Here are a few suggestions:

- ✎ a morning routine that gets children out of bed, to the breakfast table, and out the door
- ✎ an afternoon routine that includes a nap for younger children
- ✎ a "home from school" routine that requires backpacks, coats, lunch boxes, and other school paraphernalia to be put away

- ✎ a bedtime routine that helps children end their day and gets them to bed at a decent hour, allowing for ample sleep

- ✎ a vacation routine (children help pack their own bags when they are old enough, help carry things to and from the car or through airports when necessary, entertain themselves during travel time, stay close to you in airports or train terminals, and learn what to expect in terms of souvenirs and who pays for them)

- ✎ a "straightening" routine that allows each person to be responsible for picking up his or her stuff and putting it where it belongs

- ✎ a "caring for pets" routine that identifies when pet care will be done and who's responsible

I'm sure you can think of other routines that would make things more orderly in your home. If so, jot them down in the margin here so that you don't forget.

Obviously, routines change as your children age. Eventually, you'll want to help your children develop their own routines, depending on what's going on in their lives. The ability to develop and follow routines will help your children as they learn to take responsibility for their own lives. For now, creating and following routines will help create and maintain order in your home.

Step 4: Organize What You Can

If you're a Laid-Back Lackadaisical, this step will be hard for you. If you're an Organized Neatnik, feel free to jump to the next step. (You've likely already accomplished the task of organizing, and you can move on.)

This step, when combined with the next one, creates physical order in your home. This means finding a place for everything—

so that everything can be in its place. Children cannot help you keep order if they do not know where things belong. And you can't work in an orderly fashion if you're constantly looking for a place for things or searching for something that's missing.

If the thought of organizing stresses you out, or you've tried it unsuccessfully in the past, let me pass on an excellent piece of advice from a professional organizer: Focus on this day forward, rather than trying to go back and organize all the unorganized things in your home. This is why so many people's photo albums are not up to date. They think they have to go back and put all their *old* pictures in albums before they can get to *today's* photos. It's not necessary though. Simply start with your next batch of photos, and from this day forward, your pictures will be organized. The same is true of your family life. Start today, and from this day forward you'll be organized.

Being organized, *from this day forward*, does not require you to organize your closets, or your basement, or your home office (not yet, anyway). It does require you to create some sense to how you approach things. The best way to get organized (or more organized) is to ask yourself this simple question: *What isn't working?* If having ten pairs of shoes in the entryway of your home isn't working, you need a system or set of rules to govern the entryway. Perhaps each family member will be allowed to have one pair in the entryway at a time. Or perhaps you need a rack in the hall closet for family members to place their shoes. Or maybe kids should be instructed to enter your home through the garage, taking their shoes off and leaving them outside before entering your home. The important thing is that you establish a system or set of rules to organize what's not working in your home.

As you think about what's not currently working in your house, also think about this mantra: *simplify, reduce, dedicate.* These three words drive successful organization. Consider the shoes example. First, we want to *simplify* the shoe issue so that it doesn't continue to be a frustration. How can we do that? Consider *reducing* the number of shoes allowed per person in the entryway or *dedicating* space for the shoes so that they don't continue to clutter the foyer. Or maybe a combination of reducing and dedicating space would be the most effective solution.

When my son was a toddler, I was overwhelmed with the number of toys in his room. We had been using a large toy box, but it was difficult to find a specific toy without having to dig through the entire box. Using the "simplify, reduce, and dedicate" method of organizing, I opted for a shelving unit that held 13 plastic tubs. We reduced the number of toys in his room prior to employing the tubs, then dedicated them to holding his toys. I even went so far as dedicating tubs to particular types of toys: dinosaurs in one tub, Legos in another, trucks in another, and so on. The solution helped maintain toys in his room, although my plan to have each tub house a different type of toy did not stand the test of time. My original goal was met, however, since it is easier to locate toys by scanning each tub, as opposed to dumping out an entire toy box.

Earlier I suggested you ask yourself what isn't working. That simple question should drive all of your organizational efforts. A friend of mine who spent a great deal of time looking for permission slips, party invitations, and sign-up sheets solved her problem with a three-ring binder. She's *simplified* her paper organization by placing documentation for any activity her family is involved in in this *dedicated* notebook. She *reduces* the number of papers in the notebook by paging through it each week and removing those she no longer needs. As a result, she can easily find any piece of information. Her system is inexpensive and easy to use.

Let me address a myth here: Organization does not have to be expensive or difficult. While you may think you need to purchase a dozen storage bins *before* you organize your home and family, I suggest you analyze what isn't working before you spend any money. You may not need anything new after all. Instead, you might be able to reallocate space that's already being used or get rid of things by practicing the art of reduction. Instead of needing more bins for storing the clothes your children have outgrown, maybe you'll decide to get rid of the clothes altogether by taking them to a consignment shop or donating them to a charitable organization. Don't forget the value of yard and garage sales for this purpose. I know a woman who has a by-invitation open house each new clothing season to feature (and sell!) the clothes her twins have outgrown. Whatever she doesn't sell, she donates to charity.

As you begin to think about what's not currently working in your home or family life, here is one more piece of organizing advice to follow: Whenever possible, store things near where they are used. It makes it more likely they will be put away when the user is done with them.

In addition to physically organizing your space in your home, it's also important to have a system for planning (both long-term and short-term). It's stressful to have to stop on the way to a soccer game to pick up treats or to do an extra load of laundry late at night because you haven't planned ahead and your daughter needs her Girl Scout uniform tomorrow.

If you're feeling overwhelmed by the number of activities you have to manage, it's time to organize how you organize. Some of us do better taking things a day at a time, some a week at a time, and some a month at a time. I fall into this latter category. Though I usually plan a week at a time, my calendar is one in which I can see an entire month at a glance. This allows me to anticipate what's ahead without losing my focus on tomorrow.

I advocate the use of a family calendar. Ours is on the refrigerator, and all our activities are recorded there. The rule: If it's not on the family calendar, it doesn't happen. (I've been penalized myself because I failed to get something on the calendar. I learned my lesson though!) It's important that a family calendar be visible for all to see and that everything listed on it is respected as a commitment. Sometimes, tough prioritizing decisions will have to be made when it's clear the calendar is overloaded. Making commitments visible is an excellent way to train your kids to look for possible conflicts and to notify you before they happen.

Yes, organizing is an unending step. But once you get the basics of family life arranged, maintaining some semblance of order and structure gets easier.

Step 5: Anchor It

As we discussed, everything should have a place. "Anchoring it" helps you achieve the "place" goal.

At the beginning of this chapter, I shared the frustration of looking for my keys—only to find they were under the baby carrier. Up until that point, I had spent oodles of time looking for them. Sometimes they'd be in my purse, sometimes I carried them to the kitchen and set them down, and sometimes I'd put them on the washing machine as soon as I entered the house. And that was the problem: My keys did not have a home. Finding them under the baby carrier was the last straw. That day I decided to anchor them by hanging a lovely key holder my mother had given me years before. We hung a small piece of Plexiglas behind it so that the keys would not scratch the wall. Now, when I enter my home, keys are hung immediately. I'm sure I've saved several months of searching time in the future as a result of anchoring the keys!

When my daughter started school, I was at a loss as to what to do with her backpack each day when she arrived home. It usually ended up on the floor of the foyer or laundry room, neither of which has spare floor space. Should I make her carry it up to her room each night? Allow it to remain in the foyer so it would be close to the door for her departure the next day? I fretted about it. Then I hit upon a solution. I bought a small unfinished coat hanger with five large pegs, spray painted it white, and hung it in the laundry room. Instead of resting on the floor, the backpacks are hanging on the wall, out of sight of the entryway. When my daughter comes home, she heads straight to the hooks. Problem solved.

Another thing we've anchored at our house is craft items. Though we don't use them nearly as much as we used to, a large plastic tub still holds pipe cleaners, wiggly eyes, Popsicle sticks, glitter glue, children's scissors, stickers, foam shapes, and some yarn. When it's craft time, one child carries the tub over to the table, and we're ready to go.

Anchoring things simply means creating a permanent place for them, whether it be via a key holder on the wall or a backpack hanger. I've seen families with racks for athletic shoes in the garage, ball cap holders in a closet, and even Barbie Doll holders attached to the back of a bedroom door.

As you consider anchoring things, consider going vertical, as we did with the key holder and backpack rack. Using wall space in lieu of floor space is an excellent way to get more use out of limited room. I have a shoe rack that fits over the back of my closet door, which frees up the floor of my closet. Bulletin boards are a means of going vertical, as is using the front of the refrigerator to display children's art and schoolwork.

Step 6: Do It Now!

A little goes a long way when it comes to creating order in your household. In fact, once your systems are created, it should take just minutes a day to maintain them. The keys to success are not to get behind and practice the art of *doing it now!* Or at least doing it sometime *today!*

Be diligent about doing it now, and you will rarely get behind in maintaining order. Put dishes in the dishwasher after each meal rather than waiting until two or three meals have piled up. Make the beds prior to beginning your activities for the day rather than waiting until later, which often never comes. Take a few minutes to straighten the house each evening before bed, and you'll never need to do the "Big Clean-Up." Instead of thinking, "I need to straighten the family room," do it when you think of it *(now!)* instead of waiting until later. And if you can't get to the whole room right now, pick up one or two things so you get in the habit of acting when you see something that needs to be done.

I have an acquaintance who goes on periodic "straightening rampages." When she can no longer stand the clutter, she gets garbage bags and heads to her kids' rooms. She relentlessly sorts and reorganizes, assigning some things to the "toss" pile, some to the "charity" pile, and some to the "relocate" pile (which means finding a new spot for them, most likely in the basement). She hangs on to the "toss" bag for a few months, just in case her children notice something is missing. Most often, they don't.

Step 7: Involve Your Family

If you're an Organized Neatnik, you either believe it is easier to keeps things organized by doing it yourself—or you're militant about requiring your family to meet their obligations. If you're an Organized Messy, you may vacillate between doing things yourself and asking your family for help, creating confusion among family members regarding their responsibilities. If you're a Laid-Back Lackadaisical, you may think, *My family is more important than any mess!* and therefore don't involve them in keeping order. (Sometimes, you don't involve anyone in keeping order—even yourself!)

In addition to the influence of your chaos personality, you might also be influenced by the "Super Woman Syndrome"—the condition that leads you to believe you not only can, but *should*, single-handedly make life easy and convenient for every member of your family. The Super Woman Syndrome makes the mother load even heavier than it has to be. Here's how to tell if you suffer from it:

- You feel guilty when you ask family members for help.
- You think it is easier to do things yourself.
- You think it is *your* job alone as a mother to cook, clean, nurse, launder, procure food and household supplies, decorate, teach, and discipline.
- You compare yourself to other mothers who seem to keep up with everything with ease.
- You look at what you've accomplished each day and wonder why you don't get more done.
- You think mothering is easier than it actually is and don't give yourself credit for all that you do on a daily basis.

If you identified with any of these statements, you may be suffering from Super Woman Syndrome. What do you do now? The first step is acknowledgement. The second step is to ask your family for help. Doing so does not make you weak; it makes them strong. Kids need to know that the world doesn't exist to cater to them, that living in an orderly environment requires work, and that when everyone pitches in, there's less work for everybody.

Involving your family requires assigning responsibilities. Who will do what? When are they expected to do it? If you've assigned chores to your children, or they are paid an allowance for meeting specific responsibilities, you're already doing this. But asking your family for help is a fluid step, one that changes as your children mature and as your family circumstances change. How long has it been since you've evaluated the help you're getting…or *not* getting? It may be time to reassess how this is working in your family.

In addition to the regular assignments your family has, you should be able to count on periodic help as well. For example, we have a "Laundry Basket Brigade" that shows up at our house whenever things are getting out of control. Each child is given a laundry basket and asked to "drive" it around the house, searching for objects that belong to him or her. Objects are placed in the baskets, carried upstairs, and put away. This form of cleanup takes less than ten minutes. It's fun because we make it a game, and it's immensely helpful in keeping things tidy.

If your kids are younger, Barney, the big purple dinosaur, uses a cleanup song on his show. When my children were little, all I had to do was start singing the song, and they'd immediately start picking up. Perhaps you can use a similar cue for your children.

Another tactic I've used is to ask my children to pick a music CD and straighten their rooms for "as long as three songs." This is the equivalent of about ten minutes, but the time flies when the music is playing. My kids dust to music as well.

Author and mother Marie Prys also grew up cleaning to music. She recalls, "As kids we used to clean house to musicals. One of my favorite memories is of my younger sister, age seven, singing *Fiddler on the Roof's* 'If I Were a Rich Man,' word for word while dusting. We learned the classic songs this way." Though she and her siblings are all married and living in their own homes now, Marie says they all still use music when they clean house.

There is great rejoicing on my part when a child reaches a new "helping" level. My kids are now able to carry their plates from the table to the counter in order to help clear the table. That's a day I thought would never come! Though it's a little thing, it's one less thing I have to do.

Look around today and ask yourself, "How can I involve my family?" Doing so will help reduce the mother load and will teach your children the skills they'll need to one day look after themselves. The Bible advises us to "train a child in the way he should go, and when he is old he will not turn from it" (Proverbs 22:6). Helping your children learn organizing skills now will benefit them in the future.

Step 8: Take Stock

One of the most profound pieces of mothering advice I ever heard wasn't actually parenting advice at all. But it made such sense, I took it to heart as a mother. Here it is:

Stop doing what isn't working.

The counsel is so simple that I laughed when I heard it. I've applied it to child discipline, meeting my commitments, handling difficult relationships, keeping up with housework, and just about every other aspect of life.

Earlier in this chapter, I suggested you look at things that aren't working for you, then build your organizational systems around the problem areas. Now, I'm going to suggest you simply stop doing what isn't working.

When my daughter was six, she began taking dance lessons on Wednesday afternoons. She got off the bus at 3:15 and class, which was 25 minutes away, began at 3:45. Consequently, getting to class on time required a quick round of snacks and then a mad dash to the studio. This was problem number one: My daughter requires transition time between activities and hurrying stresses her out.

Problem number two: The class was taught by two high school students. Though gifted dancers, I'm not quite sure they had learned the gentle art of coaxing young, self-conscious girls who needed encouragement to drop their inhibitions and dance.

Problem number three: The class was full to the brim. Each student had approximately three square feet to dance in. My daughter prefers environments in which there are fewer people receiving more individualized attention.

I ignored all three of these problems. I wanted my daughter to dance because *I* love to dance. (There's a lesson here: This is my daughter's life, not mine. But that's another book!)

Wednesdays came and went. With each passing week my daughter became less and less interested in going to class. Eventually, she was so stressed about it that on Wednesdays, she'd step off the bus crying, knowing she'd soon be subjected to the whirlwind of getting to class on time. As her hesitation grew, my misery grew. One day, I thought to myself, *This isn't working.* And a voice in my head repeated the advice I just shared with you: Stop doing what isn't working.

Although I initially thought I was doing my daughter a favor by signing her up for dance, I realized I really was doing it because everybody else's daughter was taking dance and mine wasn't. Frankly, I was buckling under self-imposed peer pressure. None of my friends cared if my daughter took dance. But I did. I unwisely was comparing my daughter's activities to those of her friends— without properly considering her talents and interests. I learned a valuable lesson as a result.

Not wanting my daughter to be a quitter, I required her to stick with dance until the end of the calendar year, which was a convenient time to discontinue classes. We stopped doing what wasn't working, and my daughter and I are both happier as a result. Obviously, it's not possible to discontinue everything your children don't like (school, for instance!). But there are times when following the advice to stop doing what isn't working is appropriate. Doing so requires taking stock.

In addition to asking yourself what's not working in your family life, you can also take stock and become more organized by doing the following:

- Ask yourself, "What do I consistently misplace or lose?" Answering the question will show you where your problem areas are.

- Ask, "What do the kids have the most difficulty with in terms of organization?" When you solve your children's problems, you often solve some of your own.

- When you are pulled between "getting organized" and simply getting through the day, ask, "What's most important for my family as a whole right now?"

- When you become overwhelmed with the task of managing stuff and commitments, ask yourself, "Will this really matter in five years?" Pay close attention to those things that will matter. Be brave enough to let the rest go.

Taking stock is simply a tool to help you have an orderly environment. You will not, once and for all, arrive at a moment in time and space where everything is perfectly in order. You will have to continually evaluate your situation in order to respond to the changing seasons of your family's life. Taking stock enables you to see what's next in the quest to keep order. Then, unfortunately, you must UNLOAD IT all again (see beginning of chapter). And again. And again. When you do, you will discover the joy of creating order in the midst of mothering chaos.

Collecting Our Thoughts

- Our chaos personality helps identify the best approach for us when organizing.

- We don't have to manage anything we don't allow into our home or our life.

- Leading the way for our children through routines makes family life more orderly.

- Involving your family in being organized lightens the mother load.

- We need to have the courage to stop doing what isn't working.

- Effective organization requires taking stock on a regular basis and responding to the issues we identify as a result.

For Group Discussion

1. What is your chaos personality?

2. What frustrates you most about your chaos personality?

3. What's most difficult about keeping order in your home?

4. What is one thing you're proud of organizing in your home?

For Personal Reflection

1. What's not currently working in your home and/or family life?

2. In what areas can you practice "nipping it in the bud"?

3. What items are not currently anchored in your home, but need to be?

4. How can you involve your family (or involve them more) in creating and/or maintaining order in your home?

5. What one thing can you do now to help you be more organized?

What Real Live Moms Say About...
Creating Order

"I do 'impact' cleaning; for example, what five household chores can I do that will have the greatest impact on my husband when he gets home? Vacuum the floor, put away dishes, wipe the bathroom counter, pick up clutter, throw a batch of premade cookie dough in the oven."

—Angela Klinske

"I keep a master shopping list on the fridge. It lists what is in each row at the store I shop at. I circle what I need to get and can go row by row and pick it up. Works great when I need to send my husband!"

—Janet K.

"We do pick-up times (15 minutes at the end of the day and before dinner). Everyone has to have their laundry downstairs and sorted by 8:00 Monday morning or they do their own. Everyone does one load regardless. My kids each cook a meal a week and have since fifth grade. Rooms are picked up on days they have activities before they leave for their activities. I plan my meals at the beginning of the week, and my husband does the grocery shopping."

—Geriann Wiesbrook

"I created an open-top file box with hanging files to sort bills, school papers, sport papers, church papers, scouts information, invites, and personal notes to be responded to. I've found this to be *really* helpful rather than searching for notes, maps, and school calendars all over the place!"

—Trisa Johnsen

"Sometimes having a messy house is worth it if it means you get to go to your son's baseball game."

—HEATHER ADAMS

"Piles drive me crazy. I have assigned boxes for the children's 'keepers' (papers, artwork, etc.). During the school year I weed out papers weekly. I keep a sample of things they've done during the year, such as math papers, tests, journaling."

—LISA CONNOLLY

6

Meeting
Your Need for

Intimacy

I don't believe it's a coincidence that the day I was scheduled to start writing this chapter, I wasn't feeling very loving toward anyone. My husband, Stuart, and I had just been through a miserable weekend caused by conflicting priorities and expectations that had not been adequately communicated. The irony was not lost on me. The very things I was to write about in this chapter had tripped us up. I was reminded that unless pursued relentlessly, with energy and enthusiasm, intimacy is elusive. Most of us want it, but are we really willing to work for it? This question unsettles me. As I grapple with all the other aspects of the mother load, how can I also find/make time for pursuing this aspect of life? The answer is not simple, and I suspect it varies depending on one's circumstances or season of life.

What I do know is this: Intimacy provides a glimpse of who I am in relation to others and allows me to share others' reflections of who they are with them. It's through intimacy that we begin to understand ourselves and enable others to understand themselves. Knowing another, and being known, are two of life's greatest joys. It's also an integral part of God's plan.

After he created Adam, God immediately recognized that he needed to create companionship. Genesis 2:18 says, "The LORD God said, 'It is not good for the man to be alone. I will make a helper suitable for him.'" And so he did. In creating companionship, God made intimacy possible. It's his plan that we find it in our close relationships. Despite the fact that it's God's intention, creating and maintaining intimacy is a struggle. As we try to survive in today's hurry-up, "be all you can be" world, intimacy is often sacrificed. We hustle about meeting our commitments to the detriment of our inner joy, contentment, and the health of our closest relationships.

What are the intimacy busters that leave many of us feeling lonely, even when we're surrounded by others? And what can we do to encourage intimacy in our lives?

A Look at Intimacy

The American Heritage Dictionary gives us a starting point in understanding intimacy. There, we read these definitions of "intimate":

1. Marked by close acquaintance, association, or familiarity

2. Pertaining to or indicative of one's deepest nature

3. Essential, innermost

4. Characterized by informality or privacy

5. a) Very personal, private b) of or having sexual relations

Let's take a look at the first three definitions individually. The first offers valuable insight: Intimacy does not occur only between a man and a woman. This definition identifies our "intimate" relationships as those marked by closeness, such as those with our spouses, children, parents, siblings, other family members, and friends. Notice intimacy is characterized by "*close* acquaintance, association, or familiarity," thereby limiting the number of people any of us can be intimate with.

It's unrealistic to think we'll be intimate with everyone we know. This insight is valuable because it relieves us of the responsibility of seeking intimacy with everyone. In fact, it might be helpful for you to pause briefly to make a list of those you wish to be close—or closer—to. Though you can be friends with those who don't make the list, you may find that the exercise of identifying your confidants will help make your decisions about who to spend your time with easier. You might also identify friendships that have outlived their purpose in your life, thus reducing the number of people you feel beholden to.

Once we know who we want to be intimate with, the second definition helps us understand the purpose of intimacy. This definition says "pertaining to or indicative of one's deepest nature." When we are intimate with another, we open ourselves up and share our deepest nature with him or her. In turn, we discover another's deepest nature. This has been one of my greatest joys as a wife and mother: Seeing my family members' individual natures revealed and having the opportunity to contribute to those natures. In turn, I open myself up to them.

Sharing our deepest nature allows us to receive love from another, to enjoy companionship, and to experience the delight of being accepted by another (one of the most important things a parent has to offer a child and spouses have to offer to one another). More importantly, however, we have the opportunity to give all three of these things back to the people we're intimate with, thereby making a difference in their lives.

The third definition is also telling: "essential, innermost." Intimacy *is* essential. God created us to be in community with others (think back to the beginning of creation again). In order to be able to live in community successfully, we must first have a sense of our innermost self. Consequently, intimacy is not merely something we experience with others, but it's also something we experience with ourselves. Add to that the intimate relationship we should be enjoying with our heavenly Creator, and intimacy shows up in all sorts of ways in our lives. Without it, we're lonely, listless, and purposeless. With it, we live lives dedicated to serving and supporting others. In doing so, we can't help but simultaneously serve and support ourselves as well.

Though "being intimate" can refer to having sexual relations, I think it is interesting that it's the last definition in my dictionary. Understanding our spouse's deepest nature does often lead to sex. But intimacy and sex are not one and the same. It's a mistake many of us make: assuming that sex equals intimacy. It does not. For our purposes, intimacy refers to the process of building close relationships in order to glimpse another person's deepest nature and innermost being. Keep this in mind as you read. Though the ideas ahead will work with your spouse (and should definitely be used with him!), you'll also find them to be helpful in all your close relationships, including those with your children.

Intimacy Busters

It's one thing to desire intimacy, but like many other aspects of the mother load, it's hard to attain. Intimacy busters make it hard to achieve and sustain the closeness we desire with others. The following are the most common problems. Have any of these taken root in your life?

Selfishness

We live in a very me-oriented society. From an early age, we get the message that we should look out for ourselves "because if we don't, no one else will." We learn to "go for the gold," even at the expense of others. These messages are fine—if you want to live and work alone. However, they are at cross-purposes for building intimacy, which requires us to live and work with others. Doing so successfully necessitates developing the ability to put others' needs above our own—or at least equally considering them along with our own needs.

I wouldn't be writing this book if I didn't think there were times when one's own needs should take priority. As in all things though, a balance of interests is required. Intimacy requires us to consider the needs of the people around us—and to be willing to balance those needs with ours.

Selfishness is an intimacy buster because it causes us to consistently put our own wants, desires, and needs first. When we do this, we often lose the ability to consider others altogether. What starts as occasional selfishness turns into a bad habit: inflexible self-centeredness that causes us to see only what we need and want and to forget that other human beings have needs and wants, too.

Often, selfishness is a survival technique. We put others before ourselves for so long that we feel like we no longer matter. To regain our footing, we swing to the opposite side of the pendulum and refuse to put others before ourselves, causing a breakdown in our relationships.

To determine where you are on the "selfishness" pendulum, simply ask yourself if you consider others' needs *instead* of your own (you're totally unselfish), in *addition* to your own (you try to achieve a balance), or *not at all* (you're totally selfish). If you don't like how you answered this question, this may be an area for you to work on when it comes to creating and maintaining intimacy.

As we discuss the issue of selfishness, it is essential that you take a long, honest look at yourself. It's typical for partners to be very unselfish when a relationship is new and fresh. It's natural for partners to become more selfish as they settle into a routine. And, dangerously, *it's not unusual for an individual to become selfish in response to the perception that his or her needs are not being met.* In other words, if unhappiness and discontent creep into your relationship, it's natural to try to control what's happening (or to protect yourself from it), by shifting your energy from trying to please your mate to looking out for your own needs. Sometimes the shift is so subtle, it's hard to notice, especially in one's self. Are you guilty of selfishness? If so, work to banish it. There's nothing more unhappy than two people living together who are focused on their individuals needs rather than on meeting one another's needs. Intimacy cannot flourish in a relationship like this.

Silence

I admit it. I'm guilty of using the "silent treatment" to make a point in many of my relationships. All it's ever done for me, though, is to keep me focused on whatever I'm upset about. The silent treatment has never resolved a conflict, never mended a quarrel, never solved a problem, and certainly never helped me see that I was wrong. In fact, the only thing it has done is make my house quieter!

Thomas Mann wrote, "Speech is civilization itself. The word—even the most contradictory word—preserves contact. It is silence that isolates." Silence also alienates, weakens relationships, drives a wedge between two people, and makes it hard to connect with another person. If you're using the silent treatment as a weapon in your relationships, I suggest you remove it from your arsenal immediately. It can be lethal. Words not spoken can be just as damaging as those that shouldn't be spoken at all.

Douglas Weiss, Ph.D., author of *Intimacy: A 100-Day Guide to Lasting Relationships*, writes this about silence: "You are the primary voice in your spouse's life. *A silent voice is cruel.* The spouse who hears neither bad nor good from the husband or wife to whom they've committed their life feels hollow inside."[1] The same is true for our children and other loved ones.

As Thomas Mann notes, even a contradictory word (spoken in love) is better than silence, simply because it means communication, or an attempt to communicate, is occurring. Silence, when used as punishment or a means of expressing displeasure, is a powerful intimacy buster. If you need to be silent so you won't say something you regret, fine. If you need to stay silent to think something through, okay. But don't use silence to punish another person. Remember, as wives and mothers we're trying to build and encourage intimacy with our spouse and children, not destroy it.

Pressures

Time pressure. Work stress. Financial strain. Parenting anxiety. Health issues. You name it, we worry about it. Often, we lose sleep over things we can't even control. When the worries of life start pressuring us, we have a natural tendency to narrow our focus. We do this as a means of survival. But often, when we constrict our focus we lose the support our loved ones are willing to offer us. In choosing to go it alone, we miss one of the biggest benefits of intimacy: someone to walk alongside us.

Ecclesiastes 4:9-10 says, "Two are better than one, because they have a good return for their work: If one falls down, his friend can help him up. But pity the man who falls and has no one to help him up!" It's true that a worry shared is a worry lessened. Pressures should encourage us to turn toward those we are close to, rather than turn away from them. Often, we stay silent because we don't want to expose a worry or weakness. When pressures begin to build up in your life, find someone to confide in or share with. Carrying them alone often leads to *lack* of intimacy, which is why pressure is an intimacy buster.

Here's another biblical reference to tuck away for the times when the pressure's on: Matthew 6:25-27,34. These words, spoken by Jesus, are just as applicable today as they were when he first articulated them:

> Therefore, I tell you, do not worry about your life, what you will eat or drink; or about your body, what you will wear. Is not life more important than food, and the body more important than clothes? Look at the birds of the air; they do not sow or reap or store away in barns, and yet your heavenly Father feeds them. Are you not much more valuable than they? Who of you by worrying can add a single hour to his life?…Therefore do not worry about tomorrow, for tomorrow will worry about itself. Each day has enough trouble of its own.

Each day does have enough trouble of its own. And though reviewing this passage won't automatically make all your pressures go away, it will help you regain perspective. God does not give us more than we can bear, even though the pressures we experience might be great (see 1 Corinthians 10:13). When you begin to experience them, don't let them drive you away from intimacy. Instead, let them drive you closer to those you love.

Taking Others for Granted

Remember when you brought your first child home, how you'd check in the middle of the night or in the midst of an overly long nap to make sure he or she was still breathing? Eventually, after you and your infant woke up enough mornings together, you began to take for granted that you'd always wake up together. The same is true for your spouse: After waking up next to him for 15 years, you simply assume you'll have the chance to do so for another 15 years.

Taking another person for granted is perhaps the most insidious intimacy buster because it happens without our awareness and lulls us into a false sense of security. We assume that what always has been, always will be. It's the path of least resistance; the path that doesn't require any thought or any work. And that's precisely why it's so dangerous. Taking another for granted can slowly smother the flame of friendship and/or love. And often, the flame goes out without notice, and it's not until we go to warm our hands at it that we notice it is no longer burning.

Are you taking any of your loved ones for granted? If so, I encourage you to do two things right now. Make a list of five things you'd miss about this person if he or she were no longer in your life. Decide on one specific action you can take today to let him or her know how you feel. Before the sun sets tonight, let this individual know you appreciate him or her.

Because the couple relationship is central to the health of a family, it's essential that you don't take this connection for granted. This is a relationship worth protecting, which is why Genesis 2:24 counsels that a man should leave his father and his mother and be united to his wife, so that they can become one flesh. But it's also important that you don't take your relationships with your children for granted, either.

The relationships you're forging with your children right now determines what your relationship with them will look like in the future. *The openness of the relationship you'll have with them in the teen years is directly dependent on the bond you have with them now.* Don't take your children for granted now, and they are less likely to take you for granted as they get older.

Fight the urge to get comfortable in your relationships and challenge yourself not to take others for granted. More importantly, plan and implement acts of kindness that will *show* your loved ones you're not taking them for granted. Let them know you love and appreciate them.

Expecting Others to Read Your Mind

If I had a dollar for every time I thought *But I shouldn't have to tell him; he should just know* about my spouse, I'd be wealthy. Have you fallen into this trap also? It leads us to believe that "if someone really loves me, he automatically develops a way to *just know* the things he needs to know about me to keep the relationship healthy—and if he doesn't *just know*, he doesn't really love me."

What a bunch of malarkey! There are no mind readers.

The sooner you stop expecting your loved ones to read your mind, the sooner you'll be able to develop true intimacy, which is the result of fully knowing someone, not just making educated guesses about them. The only way others can truly be acquainted with you is if you're willing to communicate about yourself—your needs, wishes, dreams, and desires. If you're not willing to communicate, you'll never get what you want or need, and you'll likely be angry about it. Need I say more?

Waiting for Others to Initiate Intimacy

It would be nice if we could always expect others to harness the time, commitment, energy, and openness necessary to furthering our relationship with them. But that's unrealistic. Healthy relationships require give and take. You give some, you get some. It's true for intimacy, too. If you want to share intimate time with someone, you have just as much of an obligation to make it happen as he or she does.

Rather than waiting for others to initiate intimacy, be proactive and take the initiative yourself. Set up a lunch date, arrange for a babysitter, or feed the kids early and plan a quiet dinner. You have a choice: pine for intimacy and pout when it doesn't happen, or take the initiative to make it happen. (You'll be a lot happier if you choose the second alternative!) Be sure to applaud and encourage any attempt at intimacy by your spouse, even if it means doing something he loves and you loathe. Any time spent one-on-one or in the company of just a few others can be good for a relationship—even if it doesn't meet your expectations.

What if you're *always* the one who initiates intimacy? It's time for conversation. In a loving, nonconfrontational manner, ask for what you want. Be specific. Determine if the other person is capable and/or willing to provide it. Then, continue to do what you're doing to make sure the relationship remains a priority in your life, whether or not the other person responds. Remind yourself that you can only control your actions and act how you know you should (which is not always how you want to!).

Not Renegotiating Your Relationship After Major Life Changes

Our expectations of ourselves and others must change as our circumstances change. *Not changing expectations is not only unrealistic, it is unwise.* Time and time again, as I meet with people during my presentations and talk with them afterward, I see the effects of changed circumstances but unchanged expectations. The cancer patient who is depressed because he can't physically do what he used to be able to do because of the fatigue caused by radiation. The mother who is overwhelmed by her inability to keep up with her household chores, despite the fact that she has three young children under the age of three and is caring for an elderly parent. The man who tries to minimize the loss of a limb by pretending nothing has changed about his body or his abilities.

Not acknowledging change—and the impact it has on our lives—is unrealistic. It also seriously damages our relationships with ourselves and others.

My husband and I went through an intensely rocky period in our relationship because we weren't wise enough to renegotiate our respective responsibilities and expectations after we experienced two major life changes close together. I left full-time employment outside the home and gave birth to our second child within just a few months of each other. Assuming we could handle these changes with little or no difficulty, we kept on doing things the way we always had. Yet the change was overwhelming (more so for me than him, since so much about my life changed while he still got up every morning and went to work). Without recognizing it, we stopped working as a team and began working as individuals who just happened to share a street address. Often, our efforts were at cross purposes.

In hindsight, not talking about the changes or reassigning responsibilities was a mistake. Thankfully, with the help of a counselor, we were able to sort through the debris we accumulated as a result of these life changes and to understand how they negatively impacted our relationship. (The changes, in and of themselves, were positive. It was the effect on our relationship that was negative.) Now, when change is on the horizon, we know a renegotiation is in order.

If you've had a major life change recently and have not renegotiated your responsibilities and expectations as a result, do so as soon as possible. Relationships must be flexible and fluid in order to survive the long haul.

Anger

There is a reason that the word "anger" is one letter short of the word "danger." The two are closely related. Anger causes danger in your relationships. When you're angry, it's difficult to keep it to yourself and not let it spill over into the connections you have with other people. Consequently, unresolved anger is an intimacy buster.

I'm not suggesting you should never be angry. Anger is an emotion that serves as a compass. It warns us when danger is near. It keeps us from being taken advantage of. It tells us right from wrong. But it's unhealthy when it becomes a habit or is left over from something in the past. When that happens, anger needs to be dealt with. The sooner the better. Don't let it build up to the point of explosion. And don't let it overshadow your current relationships. How to handle anger is beyond the scope of this book. However, if anger is a problem for you, I suggest talking to a professional—either a clergy person or a trained therapist. While it may require a financial investment on your part, it's worth it to be able to wipe your slate clean and start fresh in all your relationships.

Tips for Encouraging Intimacy

By now I'm sure you're beginning to see that intimacy takes work. Sometimes a lot of it. The alternative is to do nothing and see your relationships suffer as a result. Or you can live with mediocrity in your connections with others rather than enjoying the benefits of intimacy. The irony of intimacy is this: We have to set aside our own needs and be willing to meet another's needs *before* we can get our own needs met. In other words, *we have to give the kind of love we want to get, before we can get the kind of love we want.*

Keeping this in mind, here are five tips to help you be more mindful as you seek intimacy with others.

Be a Nurturer

A nurturer is "one who provides food or other substances necessary for life and growth." Because kind and gentle words and thoughtful actions are necessary for life and growth in your relationships, a nurturer is one who speaks words of praise and affirmation.

There's a story about a woman who was contemplating ending her marriage because she believed it was loveless. She was married to a quiet, stoic man who didn't talk much or bother to share his feelings with her. She felt herself withering as a result and blamed it on her husband's shortcomings.

She prayed for God's guidance. One day, while reading her Bible, the woman came across Proverbs 25:11, which says, "A word aptly spoken is like apples of gold in settings of silver." As she pondered the imagery painted by this verse, she began to think of all the negative things she had been saying to, and about, her husband. Convicted, she decided she'd try an experiment. She'd speak only "apples of gold" (or remain quiet if she couldn't) for the next 30 days.

As the woman practiced noticing and affirming her husband, he responded by noticing and affirming her. The more she said positive things, the more he said positive things. Soon, loving gestures and acts of kindness began to flow between the two of them as a result of the verbal praise and affirmation they were sharing. The drought in their marriage was over. Before the 30-day experiment ended, the wife abandoned the idea of divorce because she had learned a simple but powerful lesson: *When you change, others change.*

Have you fallen into the criticism trap? Sometimes it's easier to come up with critical comments than it is to find words of praise that recognize another person for his or her good points. If criticism has become a habit, acknowledge it. Dennis Rainey, author of *Lonely Husbands, Lonely Wives,* reminds us that "the words you speak can affect your mate's self-esteem. Your tongue can either be a verbal ice pick that chips it away, or a paint brush that adds splashes of vibrant color by affirming and encouraging your mate."[2] Do you want your words to be cutting and cold or warm and nurturing? You have a choice. Resolve to speak only "apples of gold."

Understand the Power of Questions

In his book *The Seven Habits of Highly Effective People,* Stephen Covey suggests to his readers that they "seek first to understand, then be understood." That's good advice for anyone in a relationship. The only way to accomplish it, however, is to stop thinking about what you're going to *say,* and start thinking about what you need to *ask.* Questions serve many purposes, including building rapport, addressing conflict, getting things back on track, deflecting an attack, and preserving a relationship. More than anything, questions build bridges between people seeking to know one another intimately. Asking questions assumes you'll listen to the answers and that what you hear will lead to more questions as you connect with others.

Here's a tip to help you become more focused on asking questions. When someone says something to you, ask three follow-up questions. For example, let's say your husband comes through the door after work and says, "Geez, what a lousy day at work!" Here's how you can engage him:

> *You:* What made it so lousy?
> *Him:* Scott and Sam called in sick so I was the only one there.
> *You:* The only one?

Him: Well, Regina was there, but since she hasn't cross-trained with Scott or Sam, she really didn't know what she was doing.

You: I bet that was frustrating. Do you think they'll be back tomorrow?

What could have been answered with "Sorry to hear that" has now turned into a connection between you and your spouse. Your husband has had the opportunity to express his frustration and be heard, thus making his home a supportive haven. Open-ended questions (those that require more than a yes or no answer) are the best to keep the conversation going. Here's how such a conversation might sound with your teenager:

Her: I think my next report card is going to be bad.

You: What do you mean by bad?

Her: I mean bad.

You: Bad as in you'll never graduate from high school, or bad as in your grades aren't what you had hoped they would be?

Her: Bad as in I'm doing really poorly in math and don't understand a thing.

You: It sounds to me like you could use some help with this. Why don't we brainstorm for a couple of minutes? Then you can pick the solution you think would work for you.

See how asking questions enables you to connect with others and learn what's going on in their world? It also allow others to feel heard, an important aspect of building intimacy.

When you stop thinking about what you're going to *say*, and start thinking about what you're going to *ask*, your relationships will quickly become more intimate.

Respect Your Loved Ones

In her book *The Seven Dumbest Relationship Mistakes Smart People Make*, psychotherapist and author Carolyn Bushong advises that "to keep any relationship healthy—and especially to keep the love alive—we must accord it the respect and care we would a third person."[3] Simple but profound advice.

If you're treating the people you're *not* intimate with better than you treat those you *are* intimate with, there's a problem. And yet, all you have to do is spend time with other families to see that this is often the case in our society. Good manners force us to treat those outside our family better than those inside our family. Our familiarity with our intimates leads us to believe—falsely—that we can treat them poorly and that our closeness with them somehow makes them immune to the damage done by a lack of respect. This is a dangerous myth that leads to a gradual distancing, and in many cases, the eventual death of a relationship. Don't let it happen to you.

Use Nonverbal Communication

I'm sure you've heard the phrase "Actions speak louder than words." And it's true; they do. Even little children can understand if there's conflict between what we say and what we do. That's why congruency between your actions and words is important.

Physical touch lends weight, literally, to our words. We can say we love someone, but our words carry the most weight when our actions support them. If you were not raised in a house where hugging and kissing were the norm, this step will be difficult for you. I've seen people overcome their upbringing by making a conscious choice that they will do so. Your first attempts at introducing physical touch may be awkward for everyone involved, but they will pay dividends for years to come.

In addition to physical touch, we have eye contact to help us communicate our feelings to others. Some of my most intimate moments have come when I've had the chance to lie next to a child and stare into his or her eyes. When Marissa was born and laid on my chest for me to hold for the first time, all I could muster was the word "hello." She responded by turning her head and looking right at me. I stared into her orbs—and the eye contact we made in our first seconds together connected us deeply and continues to remind me what a precious gift I've been given. I've shared moments with Mason, too, when his eyes lock on mine and I wait for one of us to look away. Because of our comfort with one another, we can stare for a long time before that happens. The longer the stare, the more I realize how intimately we're bonded together. I pray it's a bond that will weather life's storms and last for the remainder of my existence.

Finally, we have the gift of a smile to share. Haven't some of your best moments been when you've had something to smile about—or someone to smile at? Mine have. Smiling transmits our feelings. It shows acceptance, excitement, happiness, joy, and friendliness. In short, a smile is the shortest distance between two people. When you want to connect with someone, intimately or otherwise, a smile is the quickest way to do it.

Set Aside Time

Life passes more quickly than we expect, and so does the chance to spend it with our loved ones. If we've used our time wisely, we'll be less likely to harbor regrets. Spending time with another person is one of the surest ways to pursue intimacy. Dating—even after marriage—keeps you connected with your spouse. When you don't date, your marriage becomes more of a business arrangement rather than one of intimates who choose to be together.

Since the beginning of our marriage, Stuart and I have dated, at times more successfully than others. When I look back at the tough times in our marriage, we weren't "dating." When I look back at the best times, we were. Coincidence? I don't think so. Marriage counselor Douglas Weiss offers these guidelines for successful marital dating:

1. *No problem discussions.* A date is not the time to discuss problems or personal issues about your spouse or children. By nature, a date should be fun, rather than a "gripe at your spouse" session.

2. *No money discussions.* Keep your date free of money discussions. If you need to have such a discussion, schedule a business meeting during the week.

3. *No errands.* Though errands are a necessary part of family life, running errands is not dating.

4. *Limit shopping.* Shopping leads to discussions about what to buy, instead of really talking to one another and finding out what's going on in each other's world. If you shop on a date, have it be by mutual consent. [4]

In addition to laying some ground rules, it's also important to decide how often you'll date and who will determine what you will do. Will you decide together? Take turns deciding? It's up to both of you. But make sure you come to an agreement about these issues so that dating doesn't become one more thing to argue or disagree about.

When we think of dating, we often think of something that occurs between two potential mates, but it doesn't have to be. Dating simply means spending time with someone. It's a way to pursue intimacy with anyone you care about. Who's on the date is less important than the fact that you've earmarked a time and place to be with someone you care about. I know parents who routinely have date nights with their children. I have adult friends who "date" their own parents by setting aside time to spend with them without the distraction of a spouse or children. The key is to make time for the relationships that are important in your life.

Heavenly Intimacy

The same barriers that keep us from being intimate with our loved ones on earth also keep us from being intimate with our Creator. God wants to be intimate with us, which is why he gives us the Holy Spirit. But lack of commitment, limited time, an inability to be open, and scarcity of energy all lead to a relationship with God that leaves us aching for more. In the next chapter, we'll take a look at how we can find time for spiritual growth and intimacy with the one who already knows us well, and who loves and accepts us as we are.

Collecting Our Thoughts

- God intends for us to be intimate with others.

- Achieving intimacy requires us to be deliberate, intentional, and proactive in our relationships with others.

- We have to be willing to meet another's needs before we can get our own needs met.

- Mindfulness in our relationships helps improve them. We can practice this by striving to nurture, asking questions in order to know another person better, respecting our loved ones, using nonverbal communication to affirm others, and setting aside time to be with those we desire to be intimate with.

For Group Discussion

1. Which intimacy busters are most present in your life (selfishness, silence, pressures, taking others for granted, expecting others to read your mind, waiting for others to initiate intimacy, not renegotiating your relationship after major life changes, or anger)?

2. Does intimacy come more easily with your children than it does with your spouse? Why?

3. Though most of us claim we want intimate relationships in our lives, we often don't make achieving intimacy a priority. Why is this?

4. Choose one of the "Five Steps to Encouraging Intimacy," and make a commitment to do it during the next week. Ask your group to hold you accountable.

For Personal Reflection

1. Has intimacy eluded you in your closest relationships? Why?

2. Are you as intimate with your spouse and children as you'd like to be? If not, list some steps you can take immediately to begin to restore intimacy.

3. Has intimacy become synonymous with sex in your marriage? If so, how can you add nonsexual intimacy to your rapport with your spouse?

4. In love, little things mean a lot. What little things have your family members done that meant a lot to you and let you know they love you? What little things can you do to let them know you love them?

5. How do you reveal your innermost self to those you are intimate with? If you realize you are not currently doing this, what one step can you take to begin to share yourself with those closest to you?

What Real Live Moms Say About...
Intimacy

"My husband has two questions he asks each day (from a Family Life seminar we went to together): 'Is there anything I can do for you today?' and 'Is there anything unresolved that we still need to talk about or revisit?' When he asks those questions, and we have a chance to talk, things are awesome and my intimacy needs are so met!"

—GERIANN WIESBROOK

"A man's definition of intimacy is spelled S-E-X and a woman's is spelled T-A-L-K. We compromise and have fun at it!"

—JULIE P.

"Men are not mind readers, that's for sure. In the past few years I have been very open with my husband that a hug, a kiss, or carrying the laundry upstairs for me...speak volumes of love to me. It sparks my desire for him."

—DEVONNE WHITE

"If I don't feel connected, I don't desire sex; it's that simple. But I often will accept or make advances in order to meet my husband's needs, and that will usually open the door to emotional intimacy during and afterward."

—CHRISTINE H.

"We put the kids to bed early every once in a while so that we can have some peace and quiet together. We make it a point to send the kids to Grandma and Grandpa's one day a month so we can go out on a date. We just recently started doing this, and it was amazing how much better it made our marriage. We were so caught up in being parents that we weren't very good spouses."

—REBECCA KERN

"We spent couple time socializing with other couples in an adult Sunday school class we started. Those times with other loving couples who shared the same values made a tremendously positive impact on our marriage."

—Jody Antrim

7

Meeting
Your Need for

Spiritual and
Personal Growth

One of the paradoxes of motherhood is that what we *need* as mothers is often the first thing we give up in order to *be* mothers. This is certainly true of making time for our own spiritual and personal growth. We often forego it in order to focus more fully on our children. It's a dilemma: See to your own needs or see to theirs.

Somehow, we've gotten the idea that growth has to be an either/or proposition. But the truth is, when we see to our own spiritual and personal growth, we can, by extension, see to the growth of our children. In this way, we show them the benefits of growth rather than simply talking about it. Action service instead of lip service. The "do as I do, not just as I say" style of mother leadership. Frankly, this is the toughest type of mothering there is. Tough because it requires us to lead by example.

Earlier I shared my tap dancing saga. In looking back, the experience was more than just an opportunity to spend time with friends and more than the opportunity to conquer my "tapophobia." It was, in fact, the first time since the birth of my children that I acknowledged I didn't cease to exist the moment they were born—and admitted I could continue to have a life outside my role as mom. It's a lesson my mom, Nancy Carlson, modeled for me, but until I was a mother myself, I didn't understand it.

A theater major in college, my mom continued to be active in community theater, doing one play a year so as not to lose touch with her roots. (I have fond memories of seeing her as the Blue Fairy in *Pinocchio!*) Recently, Mom shared why she did it:

> I did it to prove that there was still a "me" inside of "mother." I always made sure the homework was in process, that everyone's needs were met, then I set out to fill my own need, that of expressing myself as a person. It released the artistic angst within me, and since I felt fulfilled and alive and vibrant, I am sure I was a much better mother. I felt like I was a person in my own right. At the same time, I think, it also taught my children something about contributing to the good of our community in some small way.

A search for the "me" in mother. That's a lesson we can learn. If we're not looking for the "me" in mother, we end up simply being the "other" in mother. We don't have to give ourselves over completely to our children. It is possible to continue to exist separately *from* them, even as we are existing *for* them.

As mothers, we still have things to learn. Things to experience. Things to do. And it's important that our children know this. I personally realized this when my kids met me at the stage door after the dance recital with flowers and red licorice (my favorite!) in hand. They were proud of me and wanted to share the excitement with me. It was a touching moment: Mom the Encourager being congratulated and encouraged herself!

Though you may feel like it is impossible to make time for your own personal and spiritual growth, it's essential that you know you still matter—not because of whose mom you are (although that matters a great deal), but because of *whose* you are. You matter because you belong to God. That fact must not become obliterated because of your mothering. And it must also be passed along to your children. That's why seeing to our own growth (and by extension, theirs) is so important.

Self-growth isn't about achievement, however. It's about finding answers to questions, challenging our assumptions, learning new things, and encouraging ourselves to be different tomorrow in some way other than we are today. Sometimes, self-growth is just about living through the painful experiences that life throws our way: death, divorce, illness, or unemployment, among other things. It's being grateful for all that we have and are and making sure we're doing something with what we've been given. Self-growth is the way we show our children that life doesn't stop because we are adults—that the process of becoming who God intends us to be is lifelong.

This lesson is best shared by modeling. It may be as simple as letting your children see you reading a book. Or studying your Bible. Or looking up something in the dictionary. Or digging in your garden. Or knitting your first scarf. Or beading a bracelet. Or identifying a bird in your backyard. Or decorating a cake. Or making a soufflé. Or organizing a school party. *What* they see is not important. *That* they see it is.

Though modeling growth for your children is critical, there's another, more practical reason for this chapter. Your own growth is like a well of cool, refreshing water. When you are filled with energy, enthusiasm, excitement, and, most importantly, God's presence, you can let your kids and spouse drink from your well without worrying if there will be enough water for everyone. You *know* there will be. And though you might have to fight for the time to see to your own growth, knowing your well is full makes the fight worth it, even if you can only manage your own growth one minute at a time.

Growing with God

At the end of the last chapter, I referred to "heavenly intimacy." It's through our relationship with God that we're able to achieve this type of intimacy—and it's because of him that we have what we need (even when we don't feel like it) to meet our obligations as wives and mothers. It's a win/win situation. Time spent with God not only blesses us, it blesses those in our lives. That's all the justification we need to set aside time for our own spiritual growth even in the midst of chaos and busyness.

It's comforting to know that, despite our human failings, God places himself in each one of us when we believe in him, through the gift of the Holy Spirit. And I love how Jesus refers to the Spirit in John 16:7. He calls the Spirit "Counselor." (Other words for this are "comforter," "intercessor," and "advocate.") How reassuring to know that we have our very own comforter and counselor, especially since that's what we are to our children. Not only can we draw on God to get what we need, but we can rely on him to give us what our children need. How do we know the Spirit dwells in us? All we have to do is ask. In Luke 11:13, Jesus notes, "If you then, though you are evil, know how to give good gifts to your children, how much more will your Father in heaven give the Holy Spirit to those who ask him!"

It's not enough to ask that God dwell in you, however. Coexisting with God is one thing, but tapping into his power is quite another. It's amazing what God will do when you allow: He will enable you to see a silver lining where none existed before, empower you with just enough energy to get through the day when you feel you can't take one step more, allow you to withhold your anger when you feel like you're going to explode, and help you to laugh when you feel like crying. Perhaps most importantly, God makes it possible to hear and see and feel his guidance when you're lost and need direction.

Tapping into God's Power

Our earthly relationships benefit when we spend time with others. The same is true for our relationship with God. The more time we spend in his presence, the better we'll know him. And the better we know him, the easier it is to communicate with him and to feel his presence in our lives.

Before we go any further together, there's a myth about spiritual growth that needs to be dispelled. You do not have to wait until you have a chunk of time in order to benefit from time spent with God. I routinely take seconds to commune with him and benefit by feeling his presence in those moments, just as surely as I do when I have the luxury of an hour with him. "I don't have the time" is a lame excuse for not seeking God. Whenever you hear yourself speak those words, whether in your head or out loud, stop and redirect your thoughts. You may not have the time to sit down and do a full-fledged Bible study, but you always have the time to be in connection with God. Even a simple question like "Hi, how are you today?" leads to relationship, and that's what life with God is all about: being connected.

Thankfully, making a connection is easy. There's no telephone tag or voicemail. You won't hear, "I'm sorry, God is out of the office this week." You don't have to make an appointment, and you don't have to wait for God to get back with you. He's on call and available 24 hours a day, 7 days a week. And he doesn't take holidays or weekends off.

Following are six ways to connect with God. All are rather ordinary, but they all work. When you apply these methods, alone or in combination, you can count on a connection being made in some way, shape, or form. Here's how to tap into God's power.

Opening God's Word

Remember in grade school when you were asked to write a paper about a "historical figure"? I wrote mine about Susan B. Anthony, who played an important role in securing the right to vote for women. (I picked her because I was appalled that there had ever been a period in the history of this country when women couldn't vote. The thought still makes me shake my head in sadness and disbelief!)

Because I knew little about Susan Anthony, part of completing my assignment meant a trip to the library to learn what I could about her. As I compiled facts and figures, a picture began to emerge. This picture formed my image and understanding of this complex woman, giving me great appreciation for the sacrifices she made so that I can cast my vote on election day.

We can apply the same principles of research to learn more about God, his Son, Jesus, and the Holy Spirit. The Bible is one of our most effective methods of researching our faith. It paints a picture of our salvation, shares the stories of the early heroes of faith, reveals the nature of the Trinity, and provides excellent advice for dealing with life's ups and downs.

I personally practice three different methods of Bible study. The first is organized study, either alone or with others. This requires a Bible study guide—and the willingness to make time on my calendar to complete the work. Currently, I'm part of two women's study groups. One meets once a month, and one meets every Monday morning during the school year. We study different topics throughout the year, all with the goal of knowing God more fully. In addition to studying with others, I usually have an independent study I'm working on. Group study allows me to benefit from the insights of others, while independent study allows me to focus on a topic that may only be of interest to me.

The second type of study I'm involved in is a reading study. This is where I select a book of the Bible to read from beginning to end. No study guide is required. I read, work to understand what I've read, and then try to draw practical applications for my daily life.

The third study I do is random study. I simply sit down with my Bible, set it on its edge, let it open randomly, and begin reading where the page falls open. Often, I'm blessed by the words I read, even though they were arbitrarily selected. Or were they? I believe that God often uses the seemingly random in our lives to get a message to us. This method of study has been beneficial to me in the stormy, painful periods of my life when I'm gripped by desperation or fear and not mindful enough to be able to sit down and do a more methodical study.

Recently, I was feeling rather distant from God and lonely in my role as a mother. Bemoaning the fact that I was surrounded by people, yet still feeling alone, I let my Bible "randomly" fall open and began reading Psalm 139. Though the latter part of this psalm was familiar to me, the beginning was not. Here's what I read in the midst of my loneliness:

> Where can I go from your Spirit? Where can I flee from your presence? If I go up to the heavens, you are there; if I make my bed in the depths, you are there. If I rise on the wings of the dawn, if I settle on the far side of the sea, even there your hand will guide me, your right hand will hold me fast (verses 7-10).

As I read, my loneliness melted away. I've since committed this verse to memory so that it will be handy the next time I start feeling alone.

Though the Bible is static, the impact it has on readers is not. I can read the same passage during three different periods in my life—and get three different lessons out of it. Or I've seen different people in the same group benefit from the same message in different ways. That's the power of the Word. It meets us where we are and provides what we need when we need it. The irony is that the book must be opened before its power can work for you.

If you're not currently studying the Bible on a regular basis, find a time when you can spend a few minutes reading it. I started with a set amount of time one morning a week and have worked up from there. The important thing is that you get started. If you've never read the Bible before, I suggest starting with the Gospel of John in the New Testament. It's a good place to get a glimpse of Jesus. Then, ask God for guidance on where to go from there.

Enjoying Fellowship

In the previous chapter, we learned that God created us to be in community with others. Church is where we go to be with other believers and to worship corporately. It's also where we go to learn about faith from and with others. One of the most practical things about church is that it's an answer to the "I'm too busy" dilemma. When we make time to be at church, we mark out time for God.

There are some people who say we can worship God just as easily or effectively outside of church as we can inside. I agree with that. But this argument fails to consider two other aspects of a believer's life: what we need to hear and how we can benefit others. Church isn't just about worshiping God; it's also about hearing from him and being used by him. In other words, we never know when we'll receive guidance from him through the words of a sermon or song, the testimony of a fellow believer, the message of a skit, or a lesson in Sunday school. Because we don't know when guidance will arrive, we have to make it a priority to be open to receiving it. Attending church is one way to do this.

God uses us to encourage others in the church family, and he uses others to encourage us. But we have to be present to be used! Being present enables us to know what's going on with others, and also allows God to move through us, whether it's sharing a hug or a word of encouragement with someone who needs it, offering to babysit, lending a car, or bringing someone a home-made meal.

Church isn't just about what we get out of it. It's about worshiping God and being willing to be in service to God. When we approach church from this standpoint, we'll be pleasantly surprised by the riches God showers us with!

Connecting with God Through Prayer

At its most simple, prayer is communication with God. It can consist of a simple acknowledgement ("Hi, God!") or a lengthy, face-down plea for guidance and direction. It can be a quick "arrow prayer," when we shoot a request straight to heaven, or a monologue of praise in which we thank the Creator for all we've been given. Prayer is as different as the people who utter it.

As a child, I used to say a bedtime prayer. I knelt by my bed and recited the words I'd memorized, thanking God for his blessings and asking for his protection during my slumber. I have a confession to make. As an adult, I no longer engage in bedtime prayers for a practical reason. I fall asleep! Now, instead, I say prayers in the shower, while I prepare breakfast or clean up the kitchen, as I watch my children get on the school bus, when I exercise, while I grocery shop, in the midst of doing laundry, in the car, anywhere and everywhere I go. My prayers have turned from a once-a-day monologue to an all-day discourse. Some days I pray more than others, and some days my prayers are more organized and focused. The important thing is that I'm praying.

Prayer serves many purposes: offering praise, asking for guidance and/or forgiveness, showing thankfulness, and connecting with the Maker, to name a few. The Bible tells us to pray continually (1 Thessalonians 5:17) and to "pray in the Spirit on all occasions with all kinds of prayers and requests" (Ephesians 6:18). There is no prayer that is inadequate, too short, or improperly worded. God listens to and responds to all prayers.

As mothers, prayer is one of the most important weapons we have in our armory. It's free, has no calories, and can be used anywhere and anytime. It keeps predators at bay, enlightens us in tough mothering moments, strengthens us, provides insight and courage, and gives us direct access to our heavenly Father. The more we pray, the closer we feel to God as he begins to walk alongside us as a partner. Whether done in public with others or in private, praying is a proactive means of inviting God to move in our lives.

The Joy of Music

Whether it be the hymns of old or the praise music of today, music is another way to meet God. Either the words, or music, or both, can speak to our hearts, bring back a memory, transport us to another time and place, give us hope, offer comfort, and help us grow in our faith. Music surrounds us, fills us, touches us, and changes us. When the world swirls around us, multicolored and ever-changing, music can still us, stop us, and remind us what's important.

The popularity of Christian music is growing, and, thankfully, today we have more choices than ever to listen to. You can pick your singers, select your genre, and listen to it in many different ways including on the radio, by cable, or MP3 player. Psalm 150 tells us to praise the Lord, including praising him with music. Beginning with verse three, we read: "Praise him with the sounding of the trumpet, praise him with the harp and lyre, praise him with tambourine and dancing, praise him with the strings and flute, praise him with the clash of cymbals, praise him with resounding cymbals" (verses 3-5).

Music is one way to praise God. It's also a way to lift our hearts and spirits and to grow closer to him.

Concentrating on God

My grandparents, Ray and Mary Kierspe and Lorena and Ray Johnson, were all God-loving Christians. Our time with them always included a devotional or reading from the Bible. Though my Grandpa Kierspe has been gone for five years now, I can still hear his voice reading from his daily devotional book. This memory reminds me of how my family has been built on the firm foundation of faith. It was a privilege to sit at his feet and hear his strong voice proclaim the Word of God while my grandmother sat quietly nearby.

The tradition of devotionals continued in the home I grew up in. Though my brothers and I sometimes fought over whose turn it was to read the devotion or refused to listen if we were mad at the sibling whose turn it was to read, the existence of devotions made an impact on me. As an adult, I continue to be encouraged through devotions—quick meditations that help me focus and guide my steps.

Devotions are especially effective when we're in the season of mothering preschool children. Devotional readings are usually quick and easy to do, don't require a lot of thinking time, and some can be shared with our children. Many families read devotions together before bed or at the dinner table. Devotions are a great way to get a five-minute supercharge. And, as with many topical Bible studies, we can find teachings tailored specifically to our needs: raising teens, caring for elderly parents, building our relationship with our spouse, trying to do too much, and so forth. Find a devotional book that speaks to your heart (many are offered free of charge through churches or other charitable organizations) and take the time to read it. You'll be blessed by the words of wisdom you read and the encouragement you receive.

Spending Every Day with God

There's one method of growing closer to God that requires very little work on our part: daily living. Life is hard. Sometimes just getting through it naturally turns us toward God, whether or not we're employing any of the other methods to keep us in communion with him. But when things get tough, life can just as easily turn us *away*. We have to make a conscious decision to turn *toward* God. If we don't, inertia may interfere.

As we meet the challenge of daily living, we can actively look for evidence of God's hand on our lives. This can be achieved by pausing to look at the beauty of a flower, reflecting on how we made it through something we didn't think we could handle, or by finding the strength to love someone who seems unlovable. God is present and at work in so many ways, and yet we often fail to notice because we're in a hurry or not paying attention. I have a friend who keeps a "Gratitude Journal," in which she records the answer to prayers, the miracles she's witnessed, and the lessons she's learned on life's journey. She's shared that this is often the first place she turns when she's feeling overwhelmed because it is proof that God is at work in her life. Reviewing her notes reminds her of God's provision and has become a means of spiritual growth for her.

At my church, we have a segment in the worship service called "God Sightings." Though it only lasts a few minutes, this portion of the worship service has quickly become a favorite. Members of the congregation, as they feel moved, share experiences in which they've seen or felt God's presence in their lives. It may be an answer to prayer, a lesson learned, or an observation worth sharing. As a congregation, we're actively looking for evidence of God's work in today's world. You might want to adopt this concept for yourself and your family as you choose to make daily life one of the tools you use to grow spiritually.

The Power of Personal Growth

Seeing to our spiritual growth automatically leads to personal growth. Seeking to be closer to God allows us to see things more clearly, understand more deeply, and craft our response to the world with patience and conviction. But spiritual growth alone limits our potential. There's a whole world to explore—a wealth of things to know and learn, skills to acquire, and curiosities to satisfy. When we take time to pursue that which interests us, we ensure that we continue to grow and not stagnate. It's through this growth that we can work toward becoming the individuals God intends us to be, both now and in the future.

Many moms have ceased to exist outside of their children. They see their chief role as that of taxi driver, recreation director, tutor, cheerleader, cook, housekeeper, etiquette cop, and laundress—all rolled into one gigantic, overwhelming job that leaves no time to pursue their own interests. They forget that they were individuals before their children arrived and that they will once again exist separately from their children after the kids leave the nest. "Tomorrow" becomes their watchword. Tomorrow they'll learn to rollerblade, tomorrow they'll take up tennis again, tomorrow they'll paint their nails, tomorrow they'll call a friend, tomorrow they'll finish the cross-stitch they began before their first child was born.

Though it may be prudent to put some things on hold, it's not necessary to do it indefinitely. There comes a time when it's okay to begin to meet your own need for personal growth while you're simultaneously encouraging your children to try new things. Many of us miss this time, however, because we've put our own desires on the back burner for so long that we forget we ever even had any!

We do our children a great disservice if we make ourselves available to them 100 percent of the time. It sets up a false reality for them. If you always meet your son's needs and never make a point of meeting your own, he will grow up assuming other people will do the same for him; they will be so interested they'll drop plans and personal wants at a moment's notice to give him what he needs and what he wants. Reality hits, however, when he begins to see that other people don't exist exclusively for his benefit. The sooner our children begin to see that life is about coexistence, taking turns, negotiation, and balance, the better their chance of success in getting along with others. You're actually doing your children a favor when you pursue some of your own interests, whether it be welding, weaving, or scrapbooking.

If you're currently pursuing your interests outside of motherhood, pat yourself on the back. If not, take a minute to answer these questions:

- ∾ What things would I like to learn to do?

- ∾ What skills do I need to develop to be successful in the future?

- What am I not currently able to do that frustrates me?

- What things did I used to enjoy before I became a mother?

- What do I enjoy doing that I can share with my family?

The answers to these questions will provide a foundation from which you can actively pursue your own personal growth while mothering your children.

Nelson Mandela addressed the issue of self-growth in his inaugural speech when he became the president of the Republic of South Africa in 1994. He said, "And as we let our own light shine, we unconsciously give other people permission to do the same." Shine on, mom! In doing so, you'll encourage your children to let their lights shine as well.

Collecting Our Thoughts

- What we need as mothers is often the first thing we give up in order to be mothers.

- Time spent connecting with God not only blesses us, it also blesses those around us.

- God dwells in those who invite him in.

- You can tap into God's power through Bible study, attending church, prayer, music, devotions, and by being more intentional as you live each day.

- Pursuing your personal growth sends an important message to your children and allows you to lead by example.

170 — T<small>HE</small> M<small>OTHER</small> L<small>OAD</small>

For Group Discussion

1. Of the six methods of pursuing intimacy with God (Bible study, church, prayer, music, devotions, daily life), which is the easiest for you and why?

2. How are you growing spiritually today?

3. Share one thing you have learned as a result of abiding in God that has helped you as a mother.

4. What are you doing that will help your children know you didn't cease to exist as a person when you became a mother?

5. As you grow spiritually, what benefits can you see for your children?

For Personal Reflection

1. Which of the six methods of spiritual growth are you *not* currently employing that you could benefit from?

2. Are there changes you need to make in your schedule so you can grow spiritually (such as getting up earlier in the morning to have study time or finding a church to attend)?

3. If you've set your own personal growth aside in order to meet your responsibilities as a mother, is there a small commitment you can make now to allow yourself to enjoy activities that aren't directly related to mothering?

4. What things would you like to do before you die? (My list includes seeing the Statue of Liberty, hot air ballooning, and scuba diving on the Great Barrier Reef in Australia. I've done the first two, and I am looking forward to doing the third!) Select one item on your list and begin working to make it a reality.

What Real Live Moms Say About...
Spiritual and Personal Growth

"I find I sometimes learn more doing a toddler Bible reading or toddler devotional with my son than I do reading an adult Bible on my own. Reading from a toddler's point of view keeps it simple, has a message, and creates teachable moments."

—KIM L.

"One thing I do is I pray as I walk around the car. My kids are all buckled in. I can take a slow circle around my car and say a prayer."

—JANET K.

"I make it a huge priority to read my Bible and pray every morning. When it fits, I do a Bible study with others."

—BRANDI

"I'm in a couples' small-group Bible study, so that has continued to challenge me/grow me spiritually. I've also learned to listen to God more for instructions on how to raise my boys."

—TAMARA AHRENS

"I grow best when I combine fellowship, prayer, and Bible study. When one of these goes by the wayside, I can feel a sense of disconnection with God. My biggest challenge is finding alone time with God."

—LORI HEROLD

"When something pops into my head, I pray about it right then. I don't get to have my 'all at once' devotion times like before I was married, but I kind of like this better sometimes. God is a part of my entire day, not just…during my quiet time."

—CHRIS B.

Meeting
Your Need for
Self-Forgiveness

There are no perfect mothers—simply because there are no perfect humans. Though we know intellectually that perfection can't be achieved, for some reason many of us still think it's a mothering goal worth striving for, however elusive it may be. By deciding to be the best mother possible, we buy into the quest for perfection, and since no one is perfect, we inadvertently invite disappointment, guilt, and disillusionment into our lives.

I'm sure you have memories of moments (and maybe even entire days or seasons) that you regret in your life as a mother. Perhaps you recall losing your temper, raising your voice unnecessarily, punishing too harshly, disciplining the wrong child, or overreacting to a situation. Maybe you wish your transgressions had been as simple as those I've mentioned. Perhaps your "failure" as a mother includes worse, causing your heart to hurt with shame and humiliation at the memory.

Because our lives are so closely entwined with our children's, our failures in our roles as mothers often affect their lives, too, sometimes profoundly. When the effect is negative, it's easy to respond with guilt and a refusal to forgive ourselves. Doing so, however, affects our future effectiveness as mothers. It's a dangerous and unending cycle—until we decide we're going to break free.

There is no transgression too great not to be forgiven. (The one exception is blasphemy against the Holy Spirit—see Matthew 12:31.) God saw to that by sending his Son, Jesus, to die for our sins on the cross. He died so that we might live—fully, freely, and confidently. But in order to truly embrace God's forgiveness, we must be able to forgive ourselves. Sometimes, depending on the failure, self-forgiveness can be a tall order. But truly healthy moms are able to love and forgive themselves. In doing so, they free themselves to mother their children more fully.

The Need to Forgive

To forgive means "to excuse for a fault or offense." Self-forgiveness, then, means to excuse one's self for a fault or offense. The need for self-forgiveness arises when:

- ✎ you harm or disappoint someone, either by what you did, or by what you didn't do
- ✎ you don't live up to your own expectations of what you know you're capable of
- ✎ you've broken the moral or religious code you subscribe to

In order for self-forgiveness to be necessary, a fault or offense must occur. In order for self-forgiveness to happen, we must be able to identify that fault or offense. Often, the need for self-forgiveness is readily apparent. A wrongdoing has occurred, we know it, we repent, and we move to make amends. Other times, we're oblivious to the need for self-forgiveness because we don't recognize that we've been guilty of a fault or offense. In these cases, we may live with feelings of uneasiness, sadness, emotional discomfort, agitation, or anger without realizing why we feel the way we do. These feelings are designed to let us know we need to make amends, but as long as we harbor them without acting on them, they interfere with our ability to mother as effectively as possible. Only when an offense has been recognized, either through self-reflection or when another person tells us so, can we begin the process of forgiveness.

Recognizing the need is the first step—and perhaps the easiest step—to forgiveness. Acting on the need for forgiveness is more difficult.

A Contrast in Forgiveness

To better understand how devastating the inability to forgive oneself can be, let's take a look at two characters in the Bible, both Jesus' disciples. We'll contrast Peter, who was the leader of the disciples, with Judas, who betrayed Christ for 30 pieces of silver.

Peter was one of the first disciples called. As we learned in the earlier chapter on friendship, he was part of Jesus' inner circle of friends. When Jesus asked his followers, "Who do people say the Son of Man is?" Peter answered boldly and confidently: "You are the Christ, the Son of the living God" (see Matthew 16:13-16). Peter is also the disciple who walked on water at Christ's command (Matthew 14:26-31).

More than any other disciple, perhaps, Peter had seen with his eyes and knew with his heart that Jesus was the long-awaited Messiah. And yet, his head and heart knowledge did not keep him from denying he knew Jesus on the night the Lord was arrested, just prior to the crucifixion. Though during the Last Supper Peter tells Jesus he is ready to go with him "to prison and to death" (Luke 22:33), just hours later he denies he even knows Jesus. Let's take a look at the story, as recorded in Luke 22:54-62:

Then seizing him, they led him away and took him into the house of the high priest. Peter followed at a distance. But when they had kindled a fire in the middle of the courtyard and had sat down together, Peter sat down with them. A servant girl saw him seated there in the firelight. She looked closely at him and said, "This man was with him."

But he denied it. "Woman, I don't know him," he said.

A little later someone else saw him and said, "You also are one of them."

"Man, I am not!" Peter replied.

About an hour later another asserted, "Certainly this fellow was with him, for he is a Galilean."

Peter replied, "Man, I don't know what you're talking about!" Just as he was speaking, the rooster crowed. The Lord turned and looked straight at Peter. Then Peter remembered the word the Lord had spoken to him: "Before the rooster crows today, you will disown me three times."

And he went outside and wept bitterly.

Imagine denying knowing one of your close friends. Wouldn't the tyranny of doing so just eat you up? Imagine further that your friend was present during your denial, as Jesus was during Peter's. Though Christ may not have actually heard the words Peter used to deny knowing him, he knew it happened. Luke tells us that "the Lord turned and looked straight at Peter." Not only did Peter realize he had done wrong, but Christ knew he had, too.

I can picture Peter's eyes meeting Christ's—and the gut-wrenching realization that flooded through Peter's body as he realized he had indeed denied knowing the Messiah, just as Christ predicted. Oh, how awful that moment must have been for Peter! If there ever was a time when self-forgiveness was necessary, this was it. Peter knew he had disappointed Jesus, and the Bible tells us he "went outside and wept bitterly."

As salty tears streamed down his face, Peter had a choice: refuse to forgive himself and waste the three precious years of tutelage he received from Jesus, or forgive himself and continue to be used as a vessel of God. Thankfully, he chose the latter. It's the same decision we must make in the face of our mothering mistakes: refuse to forgive ourselves and carry a heavy burden around as a result, or free ourselves through the gift of forgiveness.

Choosing to forgive ourselves doesn't mean ignoring our shortcomings or pretending they don't exist. It does mean we'll carry on in spite of them. In the Bible, the word for forgiveness means "to abandon, send away, or leave alone." When we forgive ourselves, we choose to abandon the chokehold our mistakes have on us. We agree to move forward, as Paul wrote about in Philippians 3:14: "I press on toward the goal to win the prize for which God has called me heavenward in Christ Jesus."

Peter's ability to forgive himself paid dividends for God's kingdom. Instead of pitying himself and being crippled by his decision, he became committed to spreading the gospel. It was Peter who preached on Pentecost when 3,000 people were baptized, indicating a powerful sermon (Acts 2:14-41). Peter also introduced the gospel to the Gentiles (Acts 10) and wrote two books of the Bible (1 and 2 Peter). His ability to forgive himself empowered him and enabled him to become all that God created him to be. Self-forgiveness does the same thing for you.

Being able to forgive himself allowed Peter to make a contribution to the kingdom of heaven, rather than wasting away, remorseful and unable to function. How vivid this picture is when we compare it to that of Judas, the disciple who told the chief priests where to find Jesus the night he was arrested.

We'll pick up the story after Jesus' arrest. Matthew 27:3-5 tells us:

> When Judas, who had betrayed him, saw that Jesus was condemned, he was seized with remorse and returned the thirty silver coins to the chief priests and the elders. "I have sinned," he said, "for I have betrayed innocent blood."
>
> "What is that to us?" they replied. "That's your responsibility."
>
> So Judas threw the money into the temple and left. Then he went away and hanged himself.

Judas was not able to forgive himself for placing the love of money above his love for the Lord. As a result, he ended his life, thus stopping any good he could have done. When we refuse to pardon ourselves, we, in effect, do the same thing: limit our usefulness as God's hands on earth. Contrast that with Peter, who was able to forgive himself—and went on to be used by God in spreading the Good News.

We face a similar decision each and every time we fail in our relationship with ourselves or others. Will we "weep bitterly," then forgive ourselves and continue to be used for good? Or will we be so overwhelmed with our shortcomings that we refuse to forgive ourselves, become paralyzed, and thus become of no use to God? It's a decision we must make each and every time we fail.

The irony of Judas' choice is that the very one he betrayed came so that all people might be freed and forgiven! How sad that this truth was lost on Judas. An unwillingness to forgive yourself brings bondage and damages your ability to be as effective as possible in all your roles as a woman and as a child of

God. Self-forgiveness brings freedom, but first you must make the choice to live your life as one forgiven, as Peter did.

How Do We Accomplish Self-Forgiveness?

Self-forgiveness is comprised of three parts. The first part of forgiveness is *accepting that it is possible*. If you don't believe it is possible, you won't be able to pursue it. Thankfully, Jesus is in the forgiveness business. Because he died on the cross for you, your debt has been paid in full. As a result, you can forgive yourself for your greatest failings. That's a freeing message, but only if you're willing to embrace it and put it into action each and every time you fail. If you refuse to accept the forgiveness Jesus offers, then his death on the cross for you was for naught.

How do we know forgiveness is possible? The Bible tells us, repeatedly, that it is. First John 1:9 asserts, "If we confess our sins, he is faithful and just and will forgive us our sins and purify us from all unrighteousness." Acts 13:38 says, "Therefore, my brothers, I want you to know that through Jesus the forgiveness of sins is proclaimed to you." And Ephesians 1:7 states that "in him we have redemption through his blood, the forgiveness of sins, in accordance with the riches of God's grace."

Accepting responsibility is the second step in self-forgiveness. After you've acknowledged that forgiveness is necessary and possible, you must be willing to accept responsibility for your action(s). You cannot fully forgive yourself if you are not willing to accept responsibility for what happened. Even if you were reacting to circumstances or the behavior of another person, you still must recognize and accept the part you played. Doing so requires being honest with yourself. And be as specific as possible. If you spoke harshly to a child, acknowledge it. If you hurt someone's feelings, admit it. If you lied to your spouse, name the transgression. Though hard, this step is important. You can't be forgiven for something you don't acknowledge and accept responsibility for.

The third step is *asking for forgiveness.* By its nature, seeking forgiveness is a humbling experience because it requires confessing that you've failed in some way. At the minimum, being able to forgive yourself requires going to God, confessing your failing, and then being willing to forgive yourself. Depending on the situation, it may also mean going to the person you've injured and asking for forgiveness from them.

Although it's best to ask for forgiveness directly when possible, there are times when it is more realistic to simply forgive yourself and move on without revisiting the issue with the people involved. Perhaps the transgression happened long ago or would reopen an old wound. Or maybe the person you transgressed against doesn't even know you did it, such as when we gossip about people without their knowledge. (It's not always wise to confess our sins to people.) It's also possible that the person you hurt is no longer living or you've lost track of him or her. Regardless, you can still free yourself by communicating with God and forgiving yourself.

If the people you've transgressed against are your children, it is crucial that you admit your shortcomings to them and ask for their forgiveness for several reasons. First, doing so models healthy relationship skills to your children. Second, it shows you value them as human beings, even if they aren't yet adults. Third, it shows children that as humans we aren't perfect. We're going to make mistakes, and when we do, seeking forgiveness is the proper response. The sooner your children understand this, the sooner they begin to cultivate the skills necessary to develop healthy relationships.

If you do ask for forgiveness from another person, and he or she is not able or willing to grant it, note that *you do not need to receive forgiveness from another human being before you can forgive yourself.* God can, and will, forgive you. And you can forgive yourself, even in the absence of receiving it from another person.

When you've completed these three steps, you're forgiven. Allow yourself to learn from the mistake and move on.

What Self-Forgiveness Does

Remember "do overs" as a kid? A "do over" gives you the opportunity to try again. In my mind, self-forgiveness is like a "do over." It wipes your slate clean and lets you move ahead in your relationship with yourself and others. In addition, self-forgiveness contributes to your overall health in the following ways.

Self-Forgiveness Restores Intimacy with God

It is not possible for us to remain really close to God when we know we're doing wrong or have failed and not been willing to acknowledge it. An unwillingness to forgive shuts us off from him, sending us to a dark, lonely place. When we're willing to say "I made a mistake and I'm sorry," our close relationship with God is restored. Though he never stops loving us, we can, of our own accord, wall ourselves off from him. When we're willing to seek and grant forgiveness, however, we allow an intimate two-way relationship with the Master to resume.

Self-Forgiveness Allows Us to Let Go

If we're hanging on to regrets, disappointments, failures, shortcomings, guilt, and patterns of behavior that no longer serve us, we're hanging on to stuff that weighs us down. Forgiving ourselves is the same as dropping this baggage, regardless of how heavy it is. Those who are able to pardon themselves feel lighter and less encumbered. They are able to let go of unrealistic expectations of themselves and others and to adjust their actions as a result. They are able to let go of the past and move into the future.

Cheryl Carson, author of *Forgiveness: The Healing Gift We Give Ourselves*, tells us that even God lets go for his own sake. (Granted, God doesn't have to forgive himself, but he does practice the art of letting go.) Isaiah 43:24-25 says, "But you have burdened me with your sins and wearied me with your offenses. I, even I, am he who blots out your transgressions, *for my own sake*, and remembers your sins no more" (emphasis added). Carson writes:

> Imagine how miserable the Lord would be if he held grudges and harbored bitter, hard feelings against everyone who offended him? Everyone who took his name in vain, everyone who flaunted his counsel and his commandments, everyone who rejected his love, refused his offerings, everyone who hurt him or his beloved children in any way? He would be most miserable. So, for his own sake, he lets it go.[1]

Following God's example is good advice for us as well. Self-forgiveness lets us let go.

Self-Forgiveness Allows Us to Make Peace with Ourselves

Earlier, I mentioned some of the feelings that may accompany our refusal or inability to forgive ourselves: guilt, self-loathing, anger, pain, sadness, darkness, and isolation. Often, self-forgiveness can't come because we're wrestling with ourselves and struggling with the gap between who we are and who we want to be. This tug of war keeps us from feeling peaceful and content. A willingness to take a long, hard look at ourselves, and to see ourselves more realistically (shortcomings and all!) is the remedy to restoring peace and inner harmony. When we're able to acknowledge our shortcomings along with our strengths, we'll be able to forgive ourselves for our failings and make peace with ourselves.

Is it possible to have received forgiveness yet still feel guilty? Women I've spoken to tell me the answer is an unequivocal *yes!* If you've forgiven yourself yet still feel guilty, you've missed a step in the forgiveness process. You haven't wiped away the debt you feel you owe.

Because we've been taught that restitution must follow a transgression, many of us are in the business of punishing ourselves for our shortcomings rather than letting God deal with us. We feel we've failed, and therefore we must be punished. If you've asked for forgiveness for a failing, and you've forgiven yourself but still feel guilty, you must work at stopping the guilt in its tracks. Each time you feel it, simply say, "I've been forgiven for that, and I refuse to feel guilty." You can feel sad about what you did, regret the effect it had on others, and be determined not to repeat the transgression, but you must not let yourself continue to be haunted by guilt.

Read what Keri Wyatt Kent says about guilt in her book *God's Whisper in a Mother's Chaos:*

> Guilt is a very unproductive emotion. It's real, but feeling it doesn't get us anywhere. It doesn't inspire action but rather more guilt. God, despite the unspoken messages of many of our childhoods, is not in the "guilty" business. In fact, his central message is "not guilty: forgiven."[2]

When you feel guilty, it's important to ask if it's productive or not. If it isn't, set a time limit on it. When I have to say no to a project or activity and feel guilty as a result, I set a limit. If it's a big no, I allow myself to feel guilty for a day or two. If it's a little no, I allow myself to feel guilty for three minutes. By choosing to limit any guilt I feel, I also limit the impact it has on me.

Choosing to limit the impact guilt has is a choice to be unencumbered and as effective as possible in the future. By refusing to let guilt be your master, you open yourself up to the myriad of possibilities waiting for you. Instead of being paralyzed, you elect to be energized by the growth you're experiencing and to embrace what's ahead. You trade guilt for gladness and feeling burdened for lightness. In effect, you decline to let the mistakes of your past keep you from claiming your future.

A Final Word About Self-Forgiveness

Throughout this book I've emphasized the importance of positive modeling for our children. Repeatedly I've suggested that if you can't do something for yourself, do it for your children. The same is true with self-forgiveness.

If you refuse to forgive yourself and accept the forgiveness waiting for you, you'll miss the opportunity to let your children know that they, too, can be forgiven. Children need to hear, and see, and learn, how forgiveness works firsthand. They need to see you practice the art of forgiving yourself and others. Remember, *children learn what they live,* as well as *what they see lived out.*

When you refuse to forgive yourself, your children miss out on seeing the central part of the gospel in action. For that reason alone, moms must develop the skill of self-forgiveness. When children know forgiveness is waiting for them when they fail, they'll find the courage they need to take on the world. Giving them this courage is one of the greatest gifts you can share with them.

Collecting Our Thoughts

- Peter was able to forgive himself and produced fruit for God's kingdom as a result. We're able to do the same when we forgive ourselves.

- Judas was not able to forgive himself, which led to his death.

- Self-forgiveness comprises three parts: accepting it is necessary and possible, accepting responsibility, and asking for forgiveness.

- Self-forgiveness restores intimacy with God and allows us to let go of burdens and make peace with ourselves.

- Being forgiven doesn't immediately alleviate guilt. Often, we must actively work to overcome guilt.

For Group Discussion

1. How does guilt affect your ability to be as effective as possible as a mother?

2. Do your children sometimes try to make you feel guilty in order to get you to do what they want? If so, how do you respond?

3. What new insights did you gain in the contrast between Peter's ability to forgive himself and Judas' inability to do so?

4. Which of the three steps of forgiveness (accepting it's possible, accepting responsibility, asking for forgiveness) is toughest for you and why?

5. How does asking for forgiveness affect your self-esteem?

For Personal Reflection

1. What transgressions as a mother do you need to forgive yourself for?

2. What can you do to keep from repeating these mistakes in the future?

3. How does "mommy guilt" influence the decisions you make as a mother?

4. Do you agree with Keri Wyatt Kent that "guilt is an unproductive emotion"? Why or why not?

5. How can you model self-forgiveness for your children?

What Real Live Moms Say About...
Self-Forgiveness

"I just have to make myself step back and look at the bigger picture and not focus on the one 'small' thing that I am worrying about in order to get past the feeling of failure."

—LORI MCCLURE

"When I am really down on myself, I try to remember that God has forgiven me, and it is the epitome of arrogance to think that I know better than he. If he is willing to forgive me, I should do no less, as he is so much greater than I am!"

—MELISSA GRISSOM

"I know I've failed on many occasions. I can sometimes give myself grace for that, but as a recovering perfectionist, it's a never-ending battle."

—CHRISTINE H.

"I always evaluate and decide what I *should* have done in the situation. Just doing that helps me not continue to make the same mistakes…."

—KATHY M.

"I first ask Jesus to forgive me, and then I ask my child and/or husband to forgive me. Then, within a reasonable amount of time, I decide that if they can forgive me it's time to forgive myself."

—BRIDGET NELAN

⌒

"Going to bed at night knowing I have honestly done my best helps me forgive myself when my best just wasn't good enough. I also remember having a 'lightbulb' moment when my oldest was in junior high. I don't remember what ignited it, but I finally 'got it' that my child was a separate child of God and that she would make her own choices separate from me and that I didn't have to own all of those choices."

—JODY ANTRIM

9

Meeting
Your Need for

Laughter

The average toddler laughs 400 times per day. During that same period, the average adult only laughs 16 times. By my estimation, this means that our kids are having 25 times more fun than we are each day. Echoing what I hear frequently around my house, all I have to say is, "That's not fair!"

Indeed it's not fair. That's why this chapter is dedicated to laughter—and to making more of it bubble up in your life. Because mothering is a serious job, with serious consequences if we don't do everything "just right" (whatever that means!), many of us lose our ability to laugh freely. Some of us think we have to take ourselves seriously in order to take our work as mothers seriously. I believe that a better way to approach mothering is to take our responsibilities seriously and ourselves lightly. In order to do so, we need to learn to flex our humor muscles.

Umor is the Latin root of humor. It means "to be fluid or flowing." And "fluid" is a good word picture as we think of moms that not only survive motherhood, but also thrive. "Go with the flow" was a popular phrase some years back; it's great mothering advice as well. Our goal is to be more fluid and flexible. If we can master the art of being fluid, we'll more likely be able to see the humor that's around us every day.

And nowhere is humor more evident than around children! I kept a spiral notebook in the kitchen when my daughter, Marissa, was young so that I could capture some of the funny things she said. Here's a sampling:

- Heard after Marissa got up after falling: "Whew, I tackled myself!"

- One year, the day after Thanksgiving was warm and beautiful. Marissa walked out onto the front porch and said, "Mom, it's really bright and sunny. Come out and try it!"

- Once, after my daughter threw a fit, I said to her, "You are really misbehaving!" Confused, she replied, "I'm not misbehaving. I'm Marissa!"

- "He's the best daddy I never had!"

When I need a pick-me-up, I simply pull out this spiral notebook and read through our "family funnies." Doing so never fails to put a smile on my face. It helps me rediscover what led me to become a mother in the first place: the desire to influence and help develop another person.

I know your kids have said and done funny things, too. Unfortunately, sometimes in the midst of "funniness," we can't see it. Either we're all business when our kids are in a playful mood, or we're too overwhelmed to be able to pause long enough to look for the humor in our days. In either case, we're missing valuable opportunities to strengthen our ties with our children, reduce tension and stress, ease conflict, and create lasting memories.

Understanding the Benefits of Humor

Henry Ward Beecher, a clergyman, noted, "A person without a sense of humor is like a wagon without springs—jolted by every pebble in the road." If this is true, and I believe it is, mothers without a sense of humor are in for a rough ride simply because there are a lot of bumps on the mothering path. Humor serves as a shock absorber, making our ride smoother as we journey with our children toward the time when they'll be on their own.

Ultimately, we're not defined by our difficulties or disappointments, but how we view and respond to them. We can choose the serious response, or we can choose to ask the question, "Is there *anything* funny about this?" A spilled glass of milk isn't funny in and of itself. But if you recognize that it's not just a spilled glass of milk, but a spilled glass of milk *on a clean floor,* there's irony in the situation. You choose your response. More than once I've chosen to marvel at the timing of milk spillage in our home rather than focusing on the milk itself. Doing so allows me to laugh when I really want to cry.

In addition to buoying our spirits, laughter and joy are also gifts we give our children. I remember being about eight years old and helping my mom in the kitchen. I was mixing instant milk with water in a glass bottle. To this day, I can hear the "clink, clink" of the spoon hitting against the side of the jug as I stirred. I turned to say something to my mom and saw her eyes widen with disbelief. I turned back to the milk jug to see what she was seeing: a river of milk flowing down the counter onto the floor. I had stirred so hard that I knocked a small piece of glass out of the side of the bottle, allowing the milk to escape!

Fearing I was in trouble, I winced. My heart constricted as I waited for the lecture that was sure to come. Only it didn't. Instead, I heard my mom laugh. She knew it was an accident and chose to see the humor in the situation. Rather than punishing me, she offered forgiveness before I even asked for it. To this day I can see her eyes wide with wonder, then getting smaller as they scrunched up with laughter.

192 ~~ THE MOTHER LOAD

Several months later, my mom gifted me again when I over-whipped the whipping cream and turned it into butter. (Are you getting the picture that my skills in the kitchen are a little shaky?) She was preparing for a bridge party around the holidays. She salvaged the mistake by adding food coloring and molding the butter into the shape of a Christmas tree. (Some people turn lemons into lemonade. Not my mom. She makes Christmas trees out of butter!)

I'm not sure my mom would even remember these episodes if asked, but I certainly do. They were great lessons in mothering with grace. Because of them, I try to temper my response to my kids' failings and foibles. Our response to mishaps, however minor or major, makes a lasting impression on our children and colors how they see themselves and the world they live in. That's why we should strive to see humor in even the worst situations.

Humor as a Buffer

How we view and use humor not only affects how our kids view the world, but it can lead to more positive interactions with our children. Don't you get tired of nagging, and correcting, and repeating, and asking, and demanding, and all the other stuff you have to do as a mother? Sometimes, I flap my lips so much that I'm sure all my kids hear is garbled noise—like I'm talking under-water—coming from me. Thankfully, humor is available as a buffer when nagging is necessary.

Recently, after asking my children to hang up their coats for the umpteenth time, I changed my tactic. Instead of repeating myself, I feigned surprise and said "Mason, someone threw your coat on the floor! I wonder who did that?" Knowing full well he was the culprit, he smiled sweetly and said, "I don't know either, but I'll hang it up anyway!" This tactic was so effective I've continued to use it...with the same result each time.

Humor also helps when a child responds in an unsatisfactory manner when I ask for help or run through the agenda for the day. When I hear groans and complaints, I say, "Let's do a replay of that," and walk backward out of the room before reentering and repeating myself. If I still hear gripes and groans, I keep "rewinding" myself until the kids decide to change their response to a more positive one. My humorous approach encourages them to adjust their approach as well.

Joseph Michelli, Ph.D., author of *Humor, Play & Laughter: Stress-Proofing Life with Your Kids,* has also eliminated the negative spiral that sometimes occurs with children. He writes:

> I have made a list and numbered Andrew's most common reasons for not going to sleep. Similarly, I have listed and numbered my most common responses. Andrew has memorized his list and its corresponding number. These days, after I finish his last book, Andrew says, "Four." This means he needs a snack, to which I say, "Three," which means, "You should have gotten it earlier." For the time being, our numbers game is decreasing the nightly bedtime drama and we're having fun doing it.[1]

Humor works both ways: Not only does it help us in our interactions with our kids, but it helps them in their dealings with us and each other. I was amused recently when I heard a bit of lightheartedness parroted back to me by one of my children. The previous week, Marissa had dropped and broken a plate. Anticipating a scolding, she looked at me with hesitation to see my response. I said, "Marissa, I'm not angry. I know it was an accident." Then, smiling to confirm she wasn't in trouble, I said, "You're more important than a silly old plate!"

The next week, Marissa spilled M&Ms in the car. Before I could respond, Mason piped up and said, "It's okay, Marissa. Mom's not mad. You're more important than those silly old M&Ms!" I *was* angry, but Mason's response put my anger into perspective. My kids *are* more important than plates and M&Ms. Instead of losing my temper, as I might have done without Mason's input, I chose to make it a gentle, teachable moment instead.

Help for the Humor Impaired

I have a tendency to take things more seriously than I should. I married a man with a wonderful sense of humor though, and he's helped me learn to lighten up enough to laugh along with him. But I still consider myself to be somewhat humor impaired. My serious, goal-oriented nature gets in the way of seeing humorous happenings in the midst of my day. I'm more concerned about getting things crossed off my "to do" list than I am in lightening the mother load by laughing. So what's someone like me (and you, if you suffer from the same problem) to do when it comes to developing the ability to see more humor? I turned to several humorists (and one "jollytologist") to see what I could learn. Here's what they recommend.

Learn to Laugh at Yourself

Not only is this a valuable skill for adults, it's essential that our kids learn it, too, so they don't become the target of teasing or bullying. A person who can laugh at his or her own foibles can ward off unwanted attention and learn to let things roll off his or her back, rather than carrying a heavy load. Mastering this skill enables us to refuse to let life get the best of us. Instead, we get the best of life. This skill hit home with me one day several months after the birth of my second child. Though I'd been out of the traditional work environment for more than six months at this point, I was still doing some consulting work at home.

One day, the phone rang. I had my four-month old son in my arms as I picked it up. It was a colleague I had been hoping to hear from, offering me a contract for a speaking engagement. We spoke for several minutes as I got the details of the program. The more we talked, the more fussy my son became. Not wanting to interrupt the call, and being tethered to the wall because of the phone cord (we hadn't upgraded to cordless yet), I had to improvise. Since no one else was around, I pulled up my shirt, opened my nursing bra, and began to feed him. So far so good.

As my son began to suckle, my colleague on the phone began to give me a mailing address. Still tethered to the wall with a breast-feeding baby, I couldn't go far. I managed to grab a napkin to write on, but couldn't find a pen. So I picked up a purple crayon within reach and began to take notes. As I juggled the baby, the phone, and the crayon, my daughter started to fuss. Still not wanting to interrupt the conversation, I grabbed a few markers and dropped them on the floor at her feet. She quieted down immediately, and I carried on—and so did my colleague. On and on and on.

As the conversation stretched out, my son finished feeding, and I dutifully moved him to my shoulder to quietly burp him. As I was doing so, I glanced down at my daughter and noticed she was drawing on the wall with the markers! At the same time I realized I had failed to provide paper for her, my son threw up all over me—bright orange, stinky carrots! Mind you, I was still on the phone at this point, carrying on as if nothing was going on at my end of the phone line.

Ever the serious, consummate business professional (though I was still in my pajamas), I let my daughter continue drawing on the wall (that's what washable markers are for, right?) and finished the phone conversation with carrot slime slowly sliding down my arm. When the conversation finally ended, I said goodbye, hung up, and bowed my head in frustration. As I did, I got a picture in my mind of what this scene must have looked like from above. Feeling like I was on *Candid Camera,* I actually looked around my kitchen to see if there were any hidden cameras! Then I started to laugh. As I surveyed my carrot-soaked clothes and the marker mural on the wall, I realized how ridiculous it had been for me to carry on as if nothing was happening on my end. I was a mom pretending not to be a mom. Talk about a woman in denial!

Being covered in carrot puke was a turning point for me. I think every mom goes through it. At some point, we have to acknowledge that our priorities have changed as a result of having children, and that we, too, have changed. I could continue to try to keep up appearances and pretend I had everything perfectly under control (at the expense of my emotional health), or I could give in and admit that mothering is messy, tiring, overwhelming, frustrating, and sometimes humiliating. I chose to be honest and give in. Doing so freed me. Now, instead of worrying about what I look like or how I'm doing in the midst of mothering chaos, I focus on the fact that I'm doing it. Instead of standing on the sidelines, I'm in the game, for better or for worse. And, sister, I wouldn't trade it for anything. I know you feel the same way.

Since "The Great Carrot Episode," as I now call it, I've begun to look for the humor in even the most exasperating circumstances. The more preposterous, the better. "How would this look on *America's Funniest Home Videos?*" I ask. If there is even an inkling of humor, I allow myself to laugh. Doing so minimizes my frustration and allows me to keep a healthy perspective. It will do the same for you.

Learn to Laugh by Yourself

Due to the social nature of laughter, it occurs most often when two or more people are together. Rarely does it occur in isolation. I suspect this is because most of us feel silly laughing by ourselves. But in order to truly be able to flex our humor muscles to their fullest extent, we must be able to laugh whenever we see humor, not just when there is someone around to share it with.

I learned the value of laughing by myself many years ago when I was employed outside my home. I was going through a rather stressful period at work that required me to travel more than usual. I was trying to keep our household running, keep up with my full-time job, and excel in my role as a stepmother to my stepson, Stu. I felt like a gerbil on an exercise wheel: constantly running, but never getting anywhere.

After a particularly stressful day, during which I had to make a presentation about a controversial program, I noticed something just didn't feel right. I couldn't put my finger on it, but I was uncomfortable all day. Too hurried to figure it out, I raced through the day. That night, as I was standing in my undergarments, washing my face before bed, it dawned on me. As I looked at myself in the mirror, I could see that I had put my underwear on wrong. Instead of putting my waist through the waistline and my legs through the leg holes, I had put one leg through a leg hole, one leg through the waistline, and my waist through a leg hole! I was wearing my underwear sideways. (Not backward, mind you, but *sideways!*) The waistline flopped around one of my legs while the leg hole around my waist strained to accommodate my girth.

Although sideways underwear isn't funny in and of itself, the fact that I had stood in front of a room full of people with my underwear on wrong struck me as *very* funny. I began to laugh. With my husband just on the other side of the bathroom door, I struggled not to make noise. The more I struggled to contain myself, the funnier it got. And the funnier it got, the harder I laughed. As the first wave of laughter began to subside, I thought about how funny it was that I was in the bathroom laughing by myself. *That* tickled my funny bone all over again, and I laughed even harder. Next, I started wondering what people would think if they knew I was in the bathroom laughing alone. That thought made me laugh so hard I cried. To this day, when I think of the day I wore my underwear sideways, I still get a chuckle.

My underwear being on sideways may not be funny to you. But it was funny to me. And here's a secret about mirth: What's funny to you is funny—even if it isn't funny to anyone else. You don't need someone else to laugh with when you see something funny. Just laugh. Even if you are alone.

In 1978, *Psychology Today* magazine did a survey in which 14,500 readers rated 30 jokes. Reports author Allen Klein in his book *Healing Power of Humor*, "Not surprisingly, different people laughed at different things. 'Every single joke,' it was reported, 'had a substantial number of fans who rated it 'very funny,' while another group dismissed it as 'not at all funny.'"[2]

What's funny to you may not be funny to me, and vice versa. If you think it's funny, let yourself laugh—even if you're alone. If you don't, you'll miss a valuable opportunity to recognize humor. Since you don't know how long it will be until you see something funny again, sneak a snicker whenever you can.

Look for Humor

People with a good sense of humor have one thing in common: They are open to seeing it. When you look for humor, you're more likely to find it. Roger von Oech, author of *A Kick in the Seat of the Pants*, writes about the importance of setting our mental channel:

Take a look around where you're sitting and find five things that have blue in them. Go ahead and do it.

With a "blue" mind-set, you'll find that blue jumps out at you: a blue book on the table, a blue pillow on the couch, blue in the painting on the wall, and so on. Similarly, whenever you learn a new word, you hear it six times in the next two days. In like fashion, you've probably noticed that after you buy a new car, you promptly see that make of car everywhere. That's because people find what they are looking for. [3]

You find what you're looking for. If you're looking for humor, you're more likely to find it. If you're trudging through each day, simply hoping to get through it, you'll simply get through it. Flex your humor muscle on a regular basis, and life gets funnier. I've personally tried this tip and it works.

Smile—Even When There Is Nothing to Smile About

Psychologist Fritz Strack of West Germany is one of several researchers who have studied facial expressions on mood. Notes Strack, "It now seems clear, that facial expressions are an integral part of emotional experiences." According to Strack's research, a phony smile can trigger happy thoughts just as easily as a genuine one. "If you really want to appreciate humor," suggests Strack, "it's important that you smile—even if you have to fake it a bit."[4]

I can attest to the effectiveness of phony smiling. I have one child who smiles and laughs easily, and one, alas, who takes after me in taking things too seriously. Frequently her cherubic face is sagging with a frown. When that occurs, I make faces at her until I can get her to replace the scowl with a smile. If my funny faces don't work (and they often don't), I ask her to "practice" smiling. When she does, her mood inevitably lightens.

Comedienne Phyllis Diller was right when she said, "A smile is a curve that sets everything straight." Consequently, the best time to smile may be when you don't feel like smiling at all. The next time you're feeling blue or overwhelmed by the mother load, lighten up by smiling—even if you have to fake it.

Deterrents to Humor

Despite all that's to be gained by looking for humor, there are pesky deterrents that make it hard to find. Here are a few:

- ✍ depression
- ✍ fear
- ✍ pain
- ✍ anger
- ✍ rejection
- ✍ worry
- ✍ criticism
- ✍ anxiety
- ✍ embarrassment

Although these often keep us from being able to see the humor in our circumstances, ironically, humor is often the panacea for dealing with many, if not all, of these emotions. When we respond to unwanted feelings with a sense of humor, we can often reduce or eliminate them altogether.

As we work to help our children develop their own sense of humor, it's important to note when the negative emotions are present in their lives. Forcing a smile or expecting laughter when a child is embarrassed or anxious isn't realistic and will only serve to heighten the emotion unless, of course, we can find a way to help our child minimize the feeling through humor.

We walk a fine line in helping our children develop their humor, especially if theirs is different from ours. When it is, we must be sensitive to the differences and be careful in how we approach both humor and laughter. One child may choose to laugh *with* us while another perceives we're laughing *at* him or her. The difference between the two, which is sometimes hard to discern, is important to identify. Although humor usually heals, if used incorrectly it can also hurt. All of us can remember being the butt of a joke or the target of cruel laughter during childhood…and maybe even as recently as last week. It's an awful feeling.

Laughter is something we should share with others, not take away from them. And humor is best used to connect with others, rather than at the expense of them.

Be careful to use humor appropriately in your household, and police its use diligently. If you see that laughter is being used inappropriately, teach your children (and your spouse, if necessary) to harness it for the good it is intended for, rather than allowing them to use it destructively. Kids can be especially cruel to one another. If they are allowed to use humor inappropriately at home, it will carry over into other social settings as well. Kindness starts at home.

Developing a Humorous Approach to Life

As a parent, you have a lot to do with setting the humor tone in your household. Is laughter valued? Do you laugh and make jokes? Are you able to laugh when things go wrong, or is that not allowed in your house? How you approach humor and laughter heavily influences your children. If you're taking things too seriously and are not flexing your humor muscle enough, following are some inexpensive and easy exercises to help lighten your days.

Create a fun file where you keep funny comic strips, pictures, and other clippings. I have two favorite pictures in my humor file. One is of a principal sitting behind a child's desk, in the rain, on the roof of her school. On the ground, kids are laughing hysterically. This principal promised she'd sit on the roof if the kids read a specified number of books. They did, and she did. The picture makes me smile, which is why it ended up in my fun file.

The other picture is captioned, "Too Pooped to Pirouette." It's a shot of four-year-olds in a ballet class. Most of the students have their arms outstretched and are obviously concentrating in order to follow the teacher's instruction. One little girl, however, has her hands dropped at her sides, with her tongue hanging out of her mouth and her eyes crossed. I identified with her tired state. I've laminated this photo and have it posted on the side of my filing cabinet. Though I've had it for over a decade, I still get a kick out of it. When I'm tired, I often think to myself, "I'm too pooped to pirouette."

Treat yourself to a humorous page-a-day calendar. If nothing else, you'll increase the chance of smiling at least once each day as you turn the calendar to the current date.

Use food coloring. You read that right. Food coloring is cheap fun. Kids love green milk and squeal at blue pancakes. Blue food coloring turns bath water into marine water. Throw in small plastic sea creatures, and you've got an ocean! We've made it through plenty of L-O-N-G winter nights by turning the bathtub into Sea World.

Go to the library and leaf through Chase's Calendar of Events, a day-by-day directory of special days, weeks, and months. You'll get plenty of ideas for things you can do to lighten the mood at your house. How about observing "Eat What You Want Day" on May 11 or "Act Happy Day" on March 15? August 1-7 is "Simplify Your Life Week," something we can all benefit from. Did you know November is "National Fun with Fondue Month"? If your kids haven't had fondue yet, you certainly can have some fun with this kind of feast! There's also my personal favorite, "Talk Like a Pirate Day" on September 19. Your kids will love it when you call them "mateys" and tell them they'll have to "swab the poop deck" if they don't get their homework done.

If *Chase's* doesn't inspire you, invent your own special days, like celebrating half-birthdays (six months after one's real birthday); switch day (when parents get to be kids, and kids get to be the parents); or reverse day (where you eat dinner for breakfast and breakfast for dinner).

Borrow ideas from friends. Ask friends to share some of the humorous things they've done with their children. Author Joseph Michelli's wife adapted an idea she had heard from a friend when her son came down with chicken pox. She remembered a smock and beret in the dress-up trunk, which she donned. She concocted a mini artist's palette and became "Vincent Van Go-Away" as she painted her son with calamine lotion.[5] What are your friends doing to get giggles going at their houses? Ask. You'll get some great ideas.

Start your own "family funnies" notebook. If you're not writing down the funny things your kids are saying, start now. I know you think you'll never forget, but there have been many, many times my kids have said or done something I want to remember to share with my husband and by the time dinner rolls around, I've forgotten what it was. My mom has a notebook full of the witty, clever, and hilarious things my brothers and I said in our youth. Every couple of years we pull it out when we're all together. Doing so is always good for a laugh!

Proverbs 17:22 reminds us that "a merry heart doeth good like a medicine" (KJV). When we begin to look for and embrace the humor that's naturally present in our lives, we'll find it does our hearts good and lightens our load. Not only will we benefit, but our families will as well.

Collecting Our Thoughts

- The average toddler laughs 400 times per day. The average mother laughs only 16 times.

- *Umor* is the Latin root of humor and means "to be fluid or flowing." The goal of humor is to let things flow around and through us.

- Humor can be a buffer in our relationships with others.

- Developing a sense of humor requires learning to laugh at ourselves and by ourselves.

- We need to look for humor and smile—even when there seems to be nothing to smile about.

- How we approach humor and laughter in our lives heavily influences our children.

- Even the "humor impaired" can learn to develop their sense of humor.

For Group Discussion

1. Do you believe that moms have to take themselves seriously in order to take mothering seriously? Or can they take mothering seriously and themselves lightly?

2. Are you able to laugh freely, or do you suffer from "Seriousness Syndrome"?

3. What have you done to get the giggles at your house? Share these ideas with others in the group.

4. How does laughing with friends and family members draw us closer to them?

For Personal Reflection

1. Are you able to laugh freely when your children do something funny?

2. Which of the four steps to developing a better sense of humor would you most benefit from?

3. Think of a time when you laughed so hard you cried (or milk ran out your nose). What was it about the situation

that enabled you to laugh so freely? How can you replicate that in your home now?

4. Think of a new celebration or observance you'd like to start in your home. Note it on your calendar and begin making plans now.

5. What messages did you receive during childhood that influenced your view of humor and laughter? Are these messages valid?

What Real Live Moms Say About...
Laughter

"One morning I was flipping pancakes and my four-year-old daughter said to me, 'Mom, you don't look like an old lady today; you look pretty.'"

—KRISTINA NELSON

"My daughter got stung by a yellow jacket when she was about three and ran to tell her daddy she got stung by a 'yellow coat.'"

—CHERYL I.

"When my oldest son was about two, my husband said, 'Garrett, I'm so glad God gave you to our family.' Garrett said, 'When you were talking to him about that, did he say anything about not giving me any more spankings?' "

—LEE M.

"One time I looked at my daughter (who was about four at the time) and told her that one day she would go far. She asked me if I would come with her."

—ANGELA KLINSKE

"We were going to town, and I threw my gum out the window. Coming back, my seven-year-old said, 'What would you do if you drove by and saw a deer blowing a bubble?' "

—SUSAN DRAKE

"My second son, Micah, age six, came to me in a very distressed manner and told me that he just didn't know what to do. I asked him what was the problem. He replied, 'Mom, I just can't decide who I should marry.' I tried to assure him that he had plenty of time."

—MELISSA PINKLEY

10

Meeting
Your Need for
Help

Once, after I had organized a rather successful event while in college, a friend asked, "What are you going to do next, Mary?" Before I could reply, another friend answered: "She's going to organize the world."

Yep. That was me. Organized. In control. Self-sufficient.

And then I had kids.

Now, I'm semi-organized, sometimes in control, and no longer self-sufficient.

It's the last of these that bothers me most.

I despise having to ask for help. But more than once since becoming a mom, I've had to admit I *can't* do it on my own. It's humbling...and I don't like it. In the chapters on friendship and intimacy, we examined the fact that God created us to be in community. Intellectually, I know I need other people. But in my heart, I'm still trying to get my hands around that. To me, asking other people for help means admitting I'm not all that I should be, that I'm somehow lacking. It's a fallacy, I know, but somehow I can't get over, around, or through it.

I guess I should have known something was up when I brought my first child home from the hospital and my mother-in-law came daily to help with the cooking and to let me rest, followed by my mom who did laundry and cradled my daughter while I slept. I should have gotten the picture when friends brought food so that my husband wouldn't starve during my adjustment period from "self-sufficient" to "other efficient" and from "I am woman, hear me roar" to "I am woman, hear me whimper." Unbelievably, a neighbor I had only met once, and whose name I couldn't remember, also brought a meal—a kindness that I've never forgotten (even though her name slips my mind). That fact alone—that almost complete strangers were bringing us food—*really* should have tipped me off that something earth-shattering and life-changing had happened. Too blissful to notice, however, I charged into motherhood, confident as ever and sure I could handle whatever was to come my way.

That was my first mistake.

My second was holding on to these illusions long after I realized that's exactly what they were: erroneous perceptions of reality.

But life is changing me, and I'm now seeing that asking for help doesn't make me less than I am, but instead makes me more than who I am on my own. Weird how that works. Experts call it synergy, "the action of two or more people to accomplish what each is individually incapable of achieving." When I looked up the word "synergism" in the dictionary, I noticed there was a field note indicating a theological definition as well. I got goose bumps. *Synergism is a theological concept?* I wondered. As I read on, the goose bumps got bigger. It said, "The doctrine that regeneration is effected by a combination of human will and divine grace."

Oh my. When I ask for help, I can do more than I would be able to on my own. When I combine my human will with divine grace, I'm able to be renewed. One requires asking for earthly help; the other requires asking for heavenly help. The key to both is *asking*. And that's where the trouble starts. I stumble over the words. *I need help. Could you? Would you?* So simple, yet so hard to say.

I'm not alone. My Monday morning women's group was studying a lesson on "Serving and Being Served." We all had the serving part down pat. It was the being served we had trouble with. In fact, some of us were so impaired in this regard that we got homework assignments. We had to ask for help during the week ahead and accept it when it was offered. Then, we had to report back the next week. I did the assignment, but with a friend in the group because she already knew why I was asking.

What is it about asking for help, and accepting it, that's so hard? Here are a few thoughts:

- Asking for help means admitting we can't handle everything on our own.

- Soliciting help makes us indebted to another person.

- Requesting help means giving up control.

- We think mothering is our job and no one else's; therefore, we feel compelled to do it by ourselves.

- We don't want to burden others.

- We believe we're the only ones who can do it "right."

- We've been disappointed in the past when we have asked for help and others have let us down.

- Sometimes it's easier to do it on our own.

If you identify with any of these, I'd be willing to wager that you're carrying more of the mother load than necessary. Here's why: This thinking is narrow and limiting and, most importantly, keeps your children under your wings rather than exposing them to the broader world. As you examine your own feelings and attitudes regarding asking for help, consider the following.

Children Benefit from Having Other "Influencers" in Their Lives

My parents divorced when I was a preteen. The change in family status left me with a lot of confusion and questions. Though my mom was always patient and open when it came to listening to and answering those questions, there were some things I felt I couldn't discuss with her because I was afraid I'd hurt her feelings. My grandmother became my sounding board. While my brothers were out fishing with my grandfather, she'd sit at the kitchen table with me and listen quietly and carefully. Often, she offered advice or suggested another way of looking at the situation. Mostly she blessed me simply by listening.

My freshman year of college, I met Ted and Jane Cluett at a local church. I offered to babysit for their two young daughters—and ended up as an "adopted" daughter myself! Ted and Jane lived just minutes away from campus, and their house became a haven for me. I could study quietly there and enjoy a home-cooked meal, which I did on many occasions.

These are just three of the many, many people who have helped shape who I am. As you look back over your life, I'm sure you can name dozens of individuals who influenced you in a positive way, whether it was a neighbor, a teacher, a coach, or a family friend. We've all benefited from having people other than our parents active and interested in our lives. Your children will benefit, too—if you let them. Asking for and accepting help is one way to allow and invite other influencers into your kids' lives.

Children Used to Be Raised in Community

In the past, children were raised by a circle of caregivers, which included parents and extended family members. Now, with the average American moving every seven years and families spread across the country, it's not always possible for this to happen. Consequently, parents today are carrying a burden that was once spread among many people. Notes author Anna Quindlen, "In an odd sort of way, we feel about child-rearing the way we felt about domestic violence or sex education a decade ago: It's a private matter, to be handled at home. The weight this puts on women is enormous."[1]

When we were an agricultural society, moms simply brought their kids to work—or put the kids to work collecting eggs, milking the cow, and so forth. In many parts of the world, mothers still carry their babies on their backs, and the babies are known to, and raised by, the community as a whole.

Raising children in single-family dwellings, isolated from the greater community, is a rather new development. And though we're not likely to go back to the days of community child-rearing, we don't have to buy into the isolated way children are being raised today. Instead, we can let other people help us with our kids, and we can help them with theirs. In order to do so, we must be willing and able to get past all of the excuses mentioned previously.

The Art of Asking for Help

When I suggest that asking for help is beneficial for families, I'm not recommending that you drop your child off at a friend's for the day without reciprocating or that you ask Grandma to become a daily visitor to your home (unless both you and Grandma want her to be!). I am suggesting that you become just

214 — THE MOTHER LOAD

as diligent about meeting your own needs as you are about meeting your family's needs. Doing so requires creativity and planning. Here are some ideas to get you started.

Start Inside Your Home

At a forum for working mothers, I once heard a woman describe how her children helped around the house. Her 10-year-old did laundry, and her 14-year-old twins helped by preparing meals twice a week. At the time, I was shocked that a mother would put such young children to work! (Of course, that was before I had children of my own and before I realized how much children are capable of helping.)

Most mothers I know are good about making sure their children have chores, but they are sometimes bad at making the kids do them when it requires nagging. If you fall into the "it's easier to do it myself" trap, *stop!* You're not helping yourself, and you're not helping your children. (Fast forward to their post-school years. The habits and skills you're teaching them now will determine, in part, how successful they are on their own someday. If you're not able to accept help now because it makes *your* life easier, then be willing to accept it because someday it will make your *kids'* lives easier.)

Another valuable ally inside your home is your husband, if he is present. Though he may not naturally be as attuned as you are to knowing and/or seeing what needs to be done around the house, he still can pitch in. Like your kids and you, he can assume responsibility for weekly chores. Obviously, the workload lightens when everyone pitches in.

The key to getting help from inside your home is *asking for it*. Doing so means getting past the "it's just easier to do it myself" trap, relinquishing the "I shouldn't have to ask" mentality, and overcoming the "I'm the only one who does anything around here" martyr syndrome. If you need help, ask. Life gets simpler when you do.

Plan Ahead

Make it a practice to look ahead on your calendar in order to identify what I call "helping spots." The sooner you identify schedule conflicts, the easier it is to solve them. When a need arises, perhaps your husband can leave work an hour early or take the afternoon off. Or maybe a family member can help get everyone where they need to go. Or maybe you'll just have to plan for dinner out (or throw something into the Crock-Pot that morning) if scheduling doesn't leave time for cooking.

Anxiety is often caused by waiting until the last minute. Plan ahead and you'll minimize stress.

Reciprocate

One summer, two friends and I established a babysitting co-op. One of us would watch the kids, while the other two enjoyed the free time. We traded off each week, guaranteeing much-needed breaks during the summer. Carpooling is another excellent way to reciprocate. You drive one day, your acquaintance drives the next. Not only does this save on both gas and time, it gives you a break from your car as well!

It's easier to ask for help if you know you'll be offering your assistance in the near future. When you ask a friend to watch your kids, also ask when you can watch hers. This way, she'll have something to look forward to, and you'll have made it clear that you expect to return the babysitting favor. Another idea is to ask your husband to hang with the kids when you need him to, then volunteer to do the same for him. You can use this to your advantage.

After he goes to a friend's for *Monday Night Football*, you can get out for scrapbooking with a friend later in the week or month!

Shift Your Thinking

Common wisdom says that no one will care for your children like you. And while that's true, it's also true that there are others who will do a good job of watching your children when you're not around. If you can't bring yourself to leave the house when you have a sitter, then hire a "mother's helper," someone who will come to the house and keep your children occupied while you a) paint, b) get some work done, c) catch a catnap, or d) whatever. You pick the activity, and a sitter will make it possible for you to get it done.

My children love having babysitters. In fact, they often ask when the sitter is coming next! Having another caregiver represents a change of pace for them. Sitters focus entirely on my brood simply because they don't also have to worry about home maintenance and work commitments like parents do day in and day out. Frankly, my children enjoy the undivided attention.

If you feel selfish hiring a sitter so you can get things done, shift your thinking yet again. When I hire sitters, I see it as my way of helping *them*. I hire the sitter and the money she or he earns helps him or her a) pay for gas, b) save for college, c) buy a present for a sibling's birthday, or d) all of the above. In my book, it's a win/win situation for everyone.

Helping Yourself Help Yourself

Sometimes, we're our own worst enemies. Our preconceived notions about the way things *should* be sometimes keep us from looking at alternatives to the way things are. In a society that rewards self-sufficiency, it's hard to believe that there is any way to accomplish our goals other than relying on ourselves. But if we understand the power of synergism (the action of two or more people to accomplish what each is individually incapable of achieving), we inherently understand the benefits of accepting help to do our job as mothers. Sometimes, though, the help we need to accept is from ourselves. There are three ways we can help ourselves.

First, relinquish the idea that in order to be a "good" mother, we have to bear the bulk of child-rearing responsibilities alone. What would happen if we surrendered our need to raise our children by ourselves and, instead, accepted some help along the way? Is it possible that our children would benefit? That we would benefit? That the others we let into our kids' lives would benefit? You bet! In fact, I've seen it happen with the babysitters, physicians, Sunday school teachers, schoolteachers, neighbors, and grandparents who have touched my children's lives.

Each person my kids come into contact with offers something unique. In many cases, what they offer are things I don't provide because I don't have the skills, knowledge, or time to do so. Consequently, I need to shift my thinking from begrudgingly asking for or accepting help, to understanding the power that's unleashed when my kids are exposed to other people and other ways of doing things.

The second way we can help ourselves, and ultimately, our children, is to *give up the need to be in control*. I admitted at the beginning of this chapter that I'm a recovering control freak. So you already know that this is a tough type of surrender for me. But what about you? When it comes to children, surrendering control for safekeeping means accepting that children are not "ours"; they have been entrusted to us. We don't own them. We're responsible for clothing them, feeding them, teaching them, training them, guiding them, and loving them. We are not responsible for making them who we want them to be. Instead, it's our job to help them discover who God created them to be. And that's a freeing message—if we let it be.

Most of us have some preconceived notions about our kids: where they'll go to school, what they'll study, what kinds of jobs they might have, what salaries they'll make, what sports and instruments they'll play. Mind you, most of this is determined before a child is even born and before we know what unique skills, talents, and abilities he or she will have! Sometimes even before we know his or her likes and dislikes or what gender a child will be!

Here's a newsflash: Child-rearing isn't about molding a child into *our* preconceived notion of what he or she should be, like one would do with a bonsai tree, clipping a little here, a little there. When we try to make our children comply with our pictures for them it leads to discord and stress—on their part and on ours.

When we surrender to the idea that God has a plan for our children, as he promises in Jeremiah 29:11 (" 'For I know the plans I have for you,' declares the LORD, 'plans to prosper you and not to harm you, plans to give you hope and a future.' "), our task gets easier. Our job is simply to work with a child to help him or her discover what God's plans are, rather than trying to force-fit him or her into the preconceived notion we have.

Successful child-rearing requires us to surrender control over our children. When we do, we're more likely to be successful parents. There's less stress, and mothering gets easier and more enjoyable.

The third way we can help ourselves bear the weight of the mother load is to *accept that we were created to be just the people we are right now.* We do ourselves a disservice when we allow discontent to creep into our lives. It's hard enough meeting our responsibilities each day without the negative self-talk that often goes on in our heads. This nasty self-talk makes us want more or want what we don't have. It tells us we're stupid and lazy and makes us think we weigh too much, laugh too loud, are too short, or too something else. It leads us to believe we're inadequate and causes us to doubt our abilities as mothers.

There's a way to banish the discontent. Whenever you hear the negative little voice in your head, simply tell it you're not going to listen—not today, not tomorrow, not ever again. Instead, you're going to do what my mother made us do when we were kids. When we said something negative about ourselves or another person, she'd say, "Now, I want you tell me something positive about that person." It's a practice I'm passing along to my own children, and one I try to employ myself when the negative voice in my head starts chattering incessantly.

Here's the ultimate mothering truth: Out of all the women *in the world,* God picked you to be your kids' mom. He knew you had just what your kids needed, even with your shortcomings and quirks…and even on days when you feel like you're messing up. This thought is humbling. Even when you fail, the thought is comforting. *God picked you.* Because of that, you can soldier on, even through the most scary, disappointing, and heartbreaking mothering moments. *God picked you.* And magnificently, he'll help you when you need it in your mothering journey. Embrace this message! And pass it on to your children.

Collecting Our Thoughts

⌣ Synergy is "the action of two or more people to accomplish what each is individually incapable of achieving."

⌣ Asking for help makes us more than who we are able to be on our own.

⌣ Children benefit from having other influencers in their lives.

⌣ The key to getting help is to ask.

⌣ Good mothers don't bear all the child-rearing responsibilities alone.

⌣ Surrendering control of our children means accepting that they are not ours, but they have been entrusted to us.

For Group Discussion

1. What about asking for help is hard for you?

2. Think of a time you benefited from another person's help. How did it make you feel?

3. How do you feel when you help another person?

4. How have your children benefited from having other influencers in their lives?

For Personal Reflection

1. List the ways you are not getting help right now, and brainstorm ways to get what you need.

2. Are you benefiting your children by letting them help you, or do you fall prey to the "it's easier to do it myself" trap?

3. Have you ever been guilty of being a martyr in your family? If so, did you benefit in any way?

4. Visualize transforming "the mother load" into "the mother lode." What does "the mother lode" look like to you? Feel like? Sound like?

5. Identify one step you can take today to enable you to become more willing to ask for help.

What Real Live Moms Say About...
Help

"When I needed to tackle a big project (cleaning the basement, for example), I paid my older two in 'Internet time' to watch the younger ones. The older two had Web sites...and since their Internet time was limited to 45 minutes a day, they were more than willing to work to earn more minutes so they could work on their sites."

—BARBARA F.

"I have a couple of friends who love my boys enough to watch them for me from time to time. They love my boys and treat them like their own children. I do the same for their children. It's great for kids to have supportive adults in their lives other than their own parents."

—LEE M.

"I talk with my husband and let him know what I need. He's always willing to help out since 'if mama ain't happy, ain't nobody happy!' He helps; I'm happy; we have more time together."

—TAMARA AHRENS

"My oldest child is to take out the trash on trash day, one child is responsible for feeding and caring for the cat, and one is old enough to dust."

—KRISTINA NELSON

"I try to tag team with my husband. We help with the kids when the other person has something going on. I also share babysitting time with a friend. We watch each other's kids in order to get things accomplished."

—HEATHER V.

"I am learning how to simply ask for help rather than assuming that my husband can somehow read my mind and perceive that I need help. It's amazing what happens when you ask! People feel needed and feel a part of things instead of just spectators on the sidelines."

—CHONDRA WILLIAMS

Conclusion

After serving as a camp counselor, a Sunday school teacher, a Big Sister with Big Brothers and Big Sisters; and a stepmom, you would think that by the time Marissa and Mason came along, I would have had an idea of what to expect regarding the mother load. However, I had never parented a child from infancy on, and I was unprepared for the intensity of being needed and wanted 24 hours a day. I didn't realize how tough it would be to mother when I myself was sick; how monotonous it could be to spend hours with children coloring, playing Barbies, and creating with Play-Doh with no breaks or adult conversation; how physically exhausted I'd feel after caring for two children stricken with the Roto-virus (the symptoms are vomiting and diarrhea), which was so contagious I had to wear disposable gloves for a week while changing diapers.

Despite the fatigue, despite the tedium, despite the feeling of being frequently overwhelmed, I wouldn't give up my role of mother for anything. My life has changed for the better since knowing the joy of being called "Mom." I know the same is true for you.

Along the way, I discovered that if I were going to make it to the mothering finish line, I needed to look at this season of life as a marathon, rather than as a sprint. I needed a training regimen: a diet that would nourish my mind, body, and soul; a coach who would see me through to the finish line; and friends to cheer me on. I had to put just as much effort into being a mother as a marathoner has to put into training for a race. The ideas, training tips, and experiences mentioned in this book are helping me run the race. I know they'll do the same for you.

As I make my way down the mothering path, something else is also becoming clear: Mothers who take care of themselves have a better chance of creating lasting happiness in their families. We are the best mothers we can be when our own needs are being met. We're more patient, more loving, more energetic, more understanding, and more everything-else-we-want-to-be when our spiritual, emotional, and physical needs are being met.

God intends for you to be a joyful, fulfilled mother. He not only wants to ease your path each day, but he is willing to share and lighten your load. Allow him to. You can help by creating space in the hecticness of your days so that you can commune with him. Occasionally silence the noise in your life so that you can more clearly hear from him. And make it a priority to meet your own needs while caring for your family. Think of it as "selfless selfishness." When you are "selfish" and see to your own needs, then you can more fully be "selfless" and see to the needs of your family.

Ultimately, handling the mother load is about balance: realizing that being a good mother also means making sure your own needs are met. It's in the fullness of who you are that you can share and nurture your family. Taking care of yourself may include going for a walk when you're short-tempered and close to blowing a fuse; sitting quietly for ten minutes each day so that you can organize your thoughts and plan for tomorrow; arranging to go to your annual physical exam without children. It may mean finding the solitude necessary to call an ailing friend and talk for a few minutes; taking advantage of Mom's Night Out occasionally so your soul can be nourished and refreshed. Caring for yourself may entail enjoying time alone with your husband in order to further the relationship that began all this mothering business in the first place; creating alone time so you can benefit from a hot bath; and enjoying the blessing of quiet so that you can pray, however briefly, each day.

Coping with the mother load requires looking at all the demands placed on your life, and finding little pockets of time and space that you can use to your advantage. It requires understanding that five minutes of time alone can fuel an entire day of insane schedules, and an extra ten minutes of sleep will give you the energy you need to be at three different holiday parties during the school day, followed by three different ball fields in the afternoon.

In essence, surviving the mother load requires developing the skill of a maestro. It's your job to get all the discordant instruments in your household organized and skilled enough to make beautiful music together. It's a tough job, but when you hear the harmony that you and your family are capable of creating, it will bring joy to your soul. When you hear the music, you'll know you've transformed "the mother load" into "the mother lode." The realization will hit you in small, subtle ways: When a child slips his hand into yours; when one climbs up onto your lap and says, "I love you"; when one asks if you're going to be on the class field trip; when one confides she's having problems at school and asks for your advice; when you're the first to hear the news (both good and bad!); when you meet a fiancée and later hear the words "I do" spoken by a young adult, (your child, no less!); and when you gaze upon each of your grandchildren for the first time. That's when you'll know you've hit the mother lode. Through a series of tiny, blessed moments, you'll grasp, deeply and completely, that it's a privilege to shape and encourage another human being in a way that only a mother can do. It's in these blessed moments that we receive our mothering reward.

May God richly bless you and your family.

—Mary Byers

Notes

Chapter 1—Meeting Your Need for Solitude

1. Keri Wyatt Kent, *God's Whisper in a Mother's Chaos* (Downers Grove, IL: InterVarsity Press, 2000), 19.
2. Jim Wallis, *The Soul of Politics* (New York: Orbis Books, 1994), as quoted in Jan Johnson, *Living a Purpose-Full Life* (Colorado Springs: WaterBrook Press, 1999), 97-98.
3. Richard Foster, *A Celebration of Discipline* (San Francisco: HarperCollins, 1978), 97.
4. From *Tender Mercy for a Mother's Soul,* a Focus on the Family book published by Tyndale House Publishers. Copyright © 2001 by Angela Thomas Guffey. All rights reserved. International copyright secured. Used by permission.
5. Jan Johnson, *Living a Purpose-Full Life* (Colorado Springs: WaterBrook Press, 1999), 100.
6. Dolores Leckey, *7 Essentials for the Spiritual Journey* (New York: Crossroad Publishing Company, 1999), 43. Reproduced with permission of CROSSROAD PUBGCO (NY) in the format Trade Book via Copyright Clearance Center.
7. Foster, *Celebration of Discipline,* 108.
8. Julia Cameron, *The Right to Write* (New York: Penguin Putnam), Copyright © 1998 by Julia Cameron. Used by permission of Jeremey P. Tarcher, an imprint of Penguin Group (USA) Inc. 128.

Chapter 2—Meeting Your Need for Friendship

1. Gloria Gaither, Peggy Benson, Sue Buchanan, and Joy MacKenzie, *A Celebration of Friendship* (Grand Rapids, MI: Zondervan Publishing House, 1998), 55.
2. As quoted in Carmen Berry and Tamara Traeder, *Girlfriends: Invisible Bonds, Enduring Ties* (Berkeley: Wildcat Canyon Press, 1995), 14.
3. Ibid., 87.
4. Ibid., 20.
5. As quoted in Sandy Sheehy, *Connecting: The Enduring Power of Female Friendship* (New York: William Morrow & Company, 2000), 299.
6. Berry and Traeder, *Girlfriends,* 207.
7. Sheehy, *Connecting,* 52.
8. Annette Smith, "Tell It Like It Is," *Today's Christian Woman,* November/December 2002, 87.
9. Elisa Morgan and Carol Kuykendall, *What Every Mom Needs* (Grand Rapids, MI: Zondervan, 1995), 88.
10. Gordon MacDonald, *Restoring Your Spiritual Passion* (Nashville: Thomas Nelson, Inc., 1986), 71. Reprinted by permission of Thomas Nelson Inc. All rights reserved.
11. Angela Thomas Guffy, *Tender Mercy for a Mother's Soul* (Wheaton, IL: Tyndale House Publishing, 2001), 192-93.
12. John MacArthur, *Twelve Ordinary Men* (Nashville: W. Publishing Group, Thomas Nelson, Inc., 2002), 31, 78.

13. Joseph M. Scriven, "What a Friend We Have in Jesus," *The Worshipping Church: A Hymnal* (Carol Stream, IL: Hope Publishing Company, 1990), 622.
14. Kathleen Laing and Elizabeth Butterfield, "Need a Getaway?" *Today's Christian Woman*, May/June 2002, 44. Used by permission.
15. Camerin Courtney, "Sweet Monday," *Today's Christian Woman*, September/October 2002, 62-65.

Chapter 3—Meeting Your Need for Balance

1. Richard Swenson, M.D., *Margin: How to Create the Emotional, Physical, Financial and Time Reserves You Need* (Colorado Springs: NavPress, 1995), 83.
2. Jeff Davidson, *Breathing Space: Living and Working at a Comfortable Pace in a Sped-Up Society* (New York: MasterMedia Limited, 1991), 32.
3. Swenson, *Margin*, 85.
4. Davidson, *Breathing Space*, 26.
5. Swenson, *Margin*, 85.
6. Juliet Schor, *The Overworked American* (New York: Basic Books, 1993).
7. Charles Fishman, "Smorgasbord Generation," *American Demographics*, May 1999.
8. National Sleep Foundation. Available at: www.websciences.org/nsf/pressarchives/workforce.html and www.websciences.org/nsf/pressarchives/childrensleep.html.
9. Leslie Charles, *Why Is Everyone So Cranky?* (New York: Hyperion, 1999), 370-72. Used by permission. For more on this, go to www.WhyIsEveryoneSoCranky.com, click on "Seasonal Advice," then "Annual Theme."
10. Gordon MacDonald, *Ordering Your Private World* (Nashville: Thomas Nelson, 2003), 82. Used by permission of Thomas Nelson Inc. All rights reserved.
11. Mary LoVerde, *Stop Screaming at the Microwave* (New York: Simon & Schuster, 1998), 157-58. Used by permission.
12. Victoria Moran, *Creating a Charmed Life* (New York: HarperCollins Publishers, Inc., 1999), 45. Used by permission.

Chapter 4—Meeting Your Need for Physical Well-Being

1. Personal conversation with Susie Larson, author and speaker, Bloomington, Illinois, March 9, 2004.
2. Joe Sweeney, "Achieving a Healthy Balance in a Busy Life—Ten Minutes at a Time," *Professional Speaker,* June 2003, 15. Used by permission.
3. Joe Sweeney, http://www.joesweeney.com/articles.php#myths, accessed May 28, 2004.
4. National Sleep Foundation, http://www.sleepfoundation.org/NSAW/pk_poll resultsmood.cfm, accessed March 2, 2004.
5. Ibid., http://www.sleepfoundation.org/publications/letsleepwork.cfm, accessed April 15, 2004.

Chapter 6—Meeting Your Need for Intimacy

1. Douglas Weiss, *Intimacy: A 100-Day Guide to Lasting Relationships* (Lake Mary, FL: Siloam Press, 2001), 168, emphasis added. Used by permission.
2. Dennis Rainey, *Lonely Husbands, Lonely Wives* (Dallas: Word Publishing, 1989), 205. Used by permission.
3. Carolyn Bushong, *The Seven Dumbest Relationship Mistakes Smart People Make* (New York: Random House, 1997), 5. Used by permission.
4. Adapted from Weiss, *Intimacy*, 182-84.

Chapter 8—Meeting Your Need for Self-Forgiveness

1. Cheryl Carson, *Forgiveness: The Healing Gift We Give Ourselves* (Pleasant Grove, UT: TrueHeart Publishing, 1997), 85. Used by permission.

2. Keri Wyatt Kent, *God's Whisper in a Mother's Chaos* (Downers Grove, IL: InterVarsity Press, 2000), 56.

Chapter 9—Meeting Your Need for Laughter

1. Joseph Michelli, Ph.D., *Humor, Play & Laughter: Stress-Proofing Life with Your Kids* (Golden, CO: Love and Logic Press, Inc., 1998), 79. Used by permission.
2. Allen Klein, *The Healing Power of Humor* (Waterville, ME: Thorndike Press, 1989), 70. Used by permission.
3. Ibid., 66.
4. Ibid., 169.
5. Michelli, *Humor, Play & Laughter,* 30.

Chapter 10—Meeting Your Need for Help

1. Anna Quindlen, "Moms Shouldn't Go It Alone," *Parenting,* June/July 2003, 126.

For more information about Mary Byers' books, speaking schedule, or to share how God has used *The Mother Load* in your life, please write to:

Mary Byers
315 Bristol Road
Chatham, Illinois 62629

Or check out her website at www.marybyers.com

Hearts at Home®

The Hearts at Home organization is committed to meeting the needs of women in the profession of motherhood. Founded in 1993, Hearts at Home offers a variety of resources and events to assist women in their jobs as wives and mothers.

Find out how Hearts at Home can provide you with ongoing education and encouragement in the profession of motherhood. In addition to this book, our resources include the *Hearts at Home* magazine, the *Hearts at Home* devotional, and our Hearts at Home website. Additionally, Hearts at Home events make a great getaway for individuals, moms' groups, or for that special friend, sister, or sister-in-law. The regional conferences, attended by more than 10,000 women each year, provide a unique, affordable, and highly encouraging weekend for the woman who takes motherhood seriously.

Hearts at Home
900 W. College Ave.
Normal, Illinois 61761
Phone: (309) 888-MOMS
Fax (309) 888-4525
Email: hearts@hearts-at-home.org
Website: www.hearts-at-home.org

Other Great Books from Harvest House Publishers

The Power of a Praying® Wife
by Stormie Omartian

Bestselling author Stormie Omartian shares how you can develop a deeper relationship with your husband through prayer. Packed with practical advice on praying for specific areas, including: decision-making, fears, spiritual strength, and sexuality, *The Power of a Praying® Wife* will help you discover the fulfilling marriage God intended.

The Power of a Praying® Parent
by Stormie Omartian

Popular author and singer Stormie Omartian offers 30 easy-to-read chapters that focus on specific areas of prayers for parents. This personal, practical guide leads the way to enriched, strong prayer lives for parents.

Powerful Promises for Every Couple
by Jim and Elizabeth George

Popular Bible teacher Elizabeth George and her husband, Jim, explore 24 great promises from God, and treat each one as an individual topic that has life-changing relevance to the concerns faced by Christian couples. Includes valuable practical applications on how to benefit from each promise.

Does Your Man Have the Blues?
by David Hawkins

Depression in men—even Christian men—has reached epidemic proportions. Though clouded by secrecy and denial, depression can powerfully shape your husband's personality. He may talk and act in ways that leave you feeling unable to connect and powerless to help. Licensed clinical psychologist David Hawkins pinpoints the signs and cause of male depression and offers suggestions to help.

Being a Wise Woman in a Wild World
by Robin Chaddock
What is wisdom in our topsy-turvy world? Professional success? Becoming wonderful wives and mothers? Life coach Robin Chaddock says, "It's not about priorities and getting everything all straightened out. It's about God loving you, and you living minute by minute in that eternal love." Robin helps you know God more intimately, grasp the principles of wisdom, and put your passion and interest to work for God.

The Mother-in-Law Dance
by Annie Chapman
Can two women love the same man and still get along? Absolutely! Annie Chapman believes that a mother-in-law and daughter-in-law can become friends—even close friends. However, this connectedness is a journey. *The Mother-in-Law Dance* shares thoughtful ideas and real-life insights that will help you make your in-law relationship smooth and mutually satisfying.